# IRISH PRIDE
## 101 Reasons to Be Proud You're Irish

SONJA MASSIE

BIRCH LANE PRESS
Kensington Publishing Corp.
www.kensingtonbooks.com

BIRCH LANE BOOKS are published by

Kensington Publishing Corp.
850 Third Avenue
New York, NY 10022

First printing: 1999

10   9   8   7   6   5   4   3

Printed in the United States of America

ISBN 1-55972-488-9

# Contents

| | |
|---|---|
| Acknowledgments | viii |
| Author to Reader | ix |

PART I. ANCIENT IRELAND — 1

1. Newgrange — 3
2. Tuatha De Danann — 5
3. Ogham Stones — 7
4. The Celts — 9
5. Brehon Law — 13
6. Bardic Tradition — 15
7. Druids — 17
8. Ringed Forts — 19
9. Come to the Fair! — 21
10. St. Patrick — 23
11. St. Bridget — 26
12. Ossian and Princess Niav — 28
13. Brendan the Navigator — 31
14. The Irish Language — 33
15. Ah . . . the Scent of a Turf Fire! — 35
16. St. Columba — 37
17. The Golden Age of Ireland — 39
18. The Book of Kells — 42
19. The Tara Brooch — 44
20. The Ardagh Chalice — 46
21. Round Towers — 48
22. Brian Boru, Emperor of the Irish — 50
23. The Rock of Cashel — 53
24. Grania — 55

PART II. IRELAND'S JOYS AND WOES — 57

25. Jonathan Swift — 59
26. Irish Curses — 62

27. James Hoban 64
28. Irish Blessings 65
29. Turlough O'Carolan 67
30. Hedgerow Schools 69
31. The Gentle People 71
32. Theobald (Wolfe) Tone 73
33. Robert Emmet 75
34. The Irish "Wise" Person 78
35. Biddy Early 80
36. Thatched Cottages 82
37. Hearth and Home 84
38. Shamrocks 86
39. Daniel O'Connell 88
40. The Great Hunger 90
41. Maria Edgeworth 93
42. Irish Wit 95
43. Charles Stewart Parnell 97
44. Irish Wisdom 99
45. The Emigrants 101
46. William Butler Yeats 104
47. Ghosts of Ireland 107
48. The Abbey Theatre 109

49. The Building of America 111
50. Augusta, Lady Gregory 113
51. Sean O'Casey 115
52. George Bernard Shaw 118
53. A "Comely" People 121
54. Hurling 123
55. Oscar Wilde 125
56. Irish Insults 128
57. James McNeill Whistler 130
58. Maud Gonne 132
59. Ireland's Sons, America's
    Soldiers 134
60. John Millington Synge 136
61. Sinn Fein 139
62. John L. Sullivan 141
63. James Joyce 143
64. An Irish Wake 146
65. "A Soldier's Song" 148
66. Trinity College 150
67. Samuel Beckett 152
68. The Claddagh, Irish
    Symbol of Love 154

PART III. MODERN
      IRELAND                         157
69. The Easter Rising of
      1916                            159
70. Michael Collins                  162
71. Champions in the
      Political Arena                 165
72. Eamon De Valera                  168
73. F. Scott Fitzgerald              171
74. Irish Pubs                       173
75. Brendan Behan                    175
76. Jimmy Cagney                     178
77. Spencer Tracy                    180
78. Gene Kelly                       182
79. Irish Hospitality               184
80. John Fitzgerald
      Kennedy                        186
81. Gaelic Football                  188
82. Angela Lansbury                  190
83. Irish Setters                    192

84. Grace Kelly                      194
85. Ronald Wilson Reagan             196
86. James Galway                     198
87. Mary Higgins Clark               200
88. Makem and Clancy                 202
89. Irish Kindness                   204
90. Frank McCourt                    206
91. Tom Clancy                       208
92. Waterford Crystal                210
93. Liam Neeson                      212
94. Irish-American Cops,
      Keeping the Peace              214
95. U2                               216
96. Oral Recitation                  218
97. Seamus Heaney                    220
98. The Irish and Their
      Horses                         222
99. Irish Dancing                    224
100. The Peacemakers                 226
101. Mark McGwire                     228

# Acknowledgments

There are more than a million reasons to be proud you're Irish. But without the help of the following people, only about fifty would have been listed in this book. Thanks, guys, for everything! I love and appreciate you more than you know: Hillel Black, Laura Tucker, Bruce Hald, Blanche Hald, David Hald, and Jennifer Hald.

# Author to Reader

No doubt you've heard about the legendary "luck o' the Irish." And we *are* a fortunate people, though once you've read the course of our history, you may beg to differ. Thanks to wonderful new artists like the Riverdance performers, Enya, U2, the Cranberries, and Chumbawumba, it is now chic to be Irish, but that wasn't always the case.

Much has been said about the emerald fields of Ireland, but it is also suggested that those pastures are so green because they have been richly fed with the blood of those who struggled, lived, and perished on those beautiful but tragic sites. Throughout the history of Ireland, millions of innocent people died for no other reason than because they were Irish.

Certainly it serves no useful purpose to hate the living for the transgressions of their long-dead forefathers. A wise man once said that to hold a grudge is as foolish as swallowing a poison and expecting the other fellow to die. So why dredge up old sorrows? Why explore historical events that still have the power to shock and enrage? Because to understand any person or people, we must see where they have been to realize where they are. We must study the past to fully comprehend the present.

We Irish have 101 plus 10,000 more reasons to be proud. And a study of Irish history and tradition reveals the roots of that pride. We are far more than shamrocks, leprechauns, St. Patrick, and blarney. We are a talented, hearty, determined, compassionate, and deeply spiritual people. And we owe our rich heritage to such ancestors as the ancient Celts, the mystic Druids, the invading Vikings, the eloquent bards, and the patriotic heroes who paid the blood price so that the Ireland of today could be an independent republic.

Choosing only 101 reasons, when there are so many, was difficult. Countless extraordinary people and events were left by the wayside. Some of you may disagree with my choices; Irish folk are frequently of two minds concerning almost anything. If your favorite is not among my choices, I apologize; the slight wasn't intentional.

It was also impossible to number them according to any rating of importance. How could one decide which was more wonderful, the silver flute tones of James Galway or the athletic prowess of Mark McGwire? The logical solution was to number them chronologically, throwing in bits of Irish culture and tradition along the way. Whatever the choices and the arrangement, it is my sincere desire that you find, within these 101 essays, even more reasons to be fiercely proud of your heritage. It is, indeed, a grand thing to be a son or daughter of old Erin!

# PART 1

# ANCIENT IRELAND

# 1

# Newgrange

Contrary to the modern custom of burying in individual graves those who have died, some of the earliest inhabitants of Ireland, the Neolithic people, who migrated from Europe during the New Stone Age, probably during the fifth millennium B.C., interred their dead in community grave sites. Because of the design of these communal burial places—long, subterranean hallways or passages with small alcoves along either side to contain individual bodies—they were called "passage graves."

In the middle of the rolling hills of County Meath is one of the world's oldest mystical wonders, the passage grave site called Newgrange. Older than the oldest of Egypt's pyramids, Newgrange was erected in 3200 B.C., one thousand years before Stonehenge. It is the most remarkable of some thirty passage graves located in that vicinity.

The outside of the structure is amazing enough, an enormous mound made of 250,000 tons of rock, 36 feet high and 330 feet across. But the true wonders lie inside. The portal to the massive subterranean passage grave is marked by the Entrance Stone, an impressive rock decorated with triple swirls and strange, stylized squares. For fifty centuries the corbeled roof of the burial chamber has kept the interior dry, even during Ireland's wettest weather, and the passage, all sixty-two feet of it, remains intact, a viable corridor, leading visitors through this prehistoric wonder.

The interior is shaped like a cross and contains recesses that hold large, chiseled basins, which were used to hold the bones of the deceased buried here.

The most astonishing aspect of Newgrange is this: For 364 days a year, the mysterious passage grave remains in shadowy gloom. But on December 21, the shortest day of the year—Winter Solstice—a wonderful event occurs. At 9:45 A.M. the sun rises and light begins to creep along the passage toward the grave chamber. Minutes later, the entire interior is ablaze with the sun's rays, from the decorated side chambers to the magnificent vaulted ceiling. The marvel lasts only seventeen minutes, as it has every Winter Solstice for five thousand years. Then it is once again in shadow . . . for another year.

Newgrange remains an archeologist's puzzle. How did Stone Age man have the knowledge to assemble such a wonder? Why the Winter Solstice light phenomenon? What is the meaning of the cryptic symbols carved in stone? Perhaps it is best that we never know; after all, mystery is part of the magic of Newgrange.

# 2

# Tuatha De Danann

Thanks to the labors of medieval Christian monks, the legends of Ireland's first inhabitants were recorded for posterity. Though the line between true history and myth is blurred by the mists of time, the stories remain and continue to entertain. And some of the most loved of these tales are of the Tuatha De Danann, which translated means "the people of the Goddess Dana."

These strange, wonderful, mystical people were among the earliest of the waves of "invaders" to come to Ireland. We don't know their origins, only that they arrived by ship and burned their vessels so they wouldn't be tempted to return home. Then they wrapped themselves in a black fog and began to march inland.

They chose the site for their new settlement by releasing a swarm of bees and watching where the bees decided to call home. That spot was a plain in Tipperary named Cluan-mealla, which means "the plain of honey." There they built a *baile,* or ringed fort (see CHAPTER 8).

On the same location, a castle was later built, and it was in front of that castle, millennia after the Tuatha De Danann, that Bloody Cromwell met his greatest defeat. Two thousand of his men were killed—some say with the help of the spirits of the Tuatha De Danann.

The Tuatha De Danann were spirited fighters in life, as well. When they first arrived on the island, they battled the dark, far less civilized Firbolg for possession of the land. They were led by Nuada Lamh Airgid (Nuada of the Silver Hand), who was said to have owned a magic sword that could fight unmanned. They defeated the Firbolg in the Battle of Moytura (Plain of Towers), a spot thought to be in County Sligo. Most of the Firbolg were killed; the rest were chased to the outermost isles of the sea.

Ireland thrived under their leadership until the arrival of the Milesians, a group of Gaels from Scythia in southwest Europe. The Milesians were amazed by the spiritual culture and great mystic powers of the Tuatha De Danann. And although the militarily superior Milesians conquered the Tuatha De Danann, the Milesians continued to have great reverence for them. From that time forward, the mythology of the Milesians was based on the Tuatha De Danann, raising them above even hero status to that of gods and goddesses.

# 3

# Ogham Stones

Here and there, scattered along the side of the road in Ireland, you will see strange stones, tall rock columns with peculiar lines scratched into them.

Called Ogham stones ("Ogham" is pronounced like "poem"), they sit quietly by the roadside or in an open pasture, turning a gray face to the risings of the sun, as they have for thousands and thousands of years.

These pillar stones, called *gallans,* commemorate the dead of Ireland's ancient peoples. The word "gallan" may have come from two Gaelic words—*gol,* meaning "to cry or lament," and *lan,* which means "full." A sad term, for the marker of a sad occasion. The gallans were used in much the same way as stone gravemarkers are today. They provide a permanent record of the transient life of a human being.

Before the Christians introduced the Latin alphabet to Ireland, the only form of writing was a primitive and limited system called Ogham.

This method of writing was apparently used only to record events, such as those on the pillar stones. Ogham characters consisted of straight lines—horizontal, vertical, and slanted—that could easily be scratched or carved into rock.

Since the Celtic tradition placed great emphasis on oral tradition, rather than written records, the need for a more formal, versatile alphabet was unnecessary. The Druid poets of the day were not inclined to put their secrets into writing, where they could be seen and studied by everyone. Instead, they taught their disciples personally, through oral recitation, and their words stayed strictly between those who studied the esoteric practices.

Only the arrival of the Latin alphabet, brought by the Christian monks in the mid-400s A.D., would change the ancient ways of the Druids and the need for the primitive writing found on the Ogham stones, thus creating a whole new world of communication for scholars and poets.

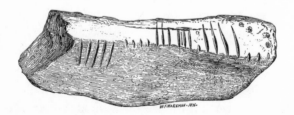

# 4

# The Celts

## (European Invasion Approx. 500–300 B.C.)

The very word *Celt* (from the Greek word *Keltoi*) means "barbarian." So it might not be immediately obvious why we Irish would take pride in these ancestors, who were reputed to be some of the most savage people in the world's history. But the Celts, while a fierce, hedonistic, war-mongering society, were a complex people and had one of the most advanced civilizations in ancient times.

Many of the most endearing aspects of the contemporary Irish character can be attributed to these colorful, controversial forebears of the Irish people. They, too, had a deep reverence for the law (see CHAPTER 5), for storytelling (see CHAPTER 6), for education, and for the arts.

The Celts were not a pure race, but rather a conglomeration of tribes with a common language and a mutual love of conquest. Generally speaking, they were an attractive people, light-skinned and longer limbed than most people of those days. They had fair hair, which they wore in wild manes, streaming down their backs.

Originally from the region of the Volga steppes in western Russia, the Celts were among the first humans to domesticate the horse (around 3000 B.C.), using it for plowing and for transportation. They were also advanced for their day in metalworking, particularly the use of iron in weaponry. Having invented chain mail and developed an arsenal of extremely effective slashing swords, protective helmets, large shields, and innovative body armor, they were far superior militarily to their European neighbors.

Around 500 B.C., the Celts began to conduct occasional raids into Europe. They were fearsome warriors who would work themselves into a frenzy before battle, to the point where they would often throw off their armor and ride naked, shrieking, blowing horns, and clanging their swords against their shields as they descended upon their victims.

The Celts had no fear of battle or death. A belief in reincarnation taught them that death was nothing more than a portal to the next life. And there was no more glorious way to pass from one existence to the other than to die on the battlefield.

Once the Celts discovered that their European neighbors were easy prey, they began a campaign to conquer the entire continent. They were highly successful; by 300 B.C. they controlled everything from Finisterre to the Black Sea and from the North Sea to the Mediterranean.

The Celts subdued other societies both by force and by assimilation. They took wives from among the natives and adopted whatever aspects of those cultures appealed to them. From India, they took the idea of a caste system, in which every member of society knew his place, his occupation, his responsibilities, and his privileges. From the Germanic peoples, they embraced the concept of charging fines for crimes, rather than imprisoning the offenders (see CHAPTER 5).

Though it may seem like a contradiction, the same people who hung the severed heads of their enemies from their horses' necks also considered education vital. The Druids were a sect of the Celtic society who functioned as spiritual leaders, mystics, and seers, but they also fulfilled the role of teachers in such areas of knowledge as genealogies, mythology, astronomy, mathematics, geography, and the Druidic religion and its secret rituals. Education was held in such high esteem by the Celts that the keepers of knowledge, the Druids—storytelling bards and poets—held as prestigious a position as kings.

The Celts were also fiercely individualistic. Each man considered himself important, not just as a functioning member of his society but as a valuable entity in his own right. Personal decoration was a meaningful form of expression to the Celts, and great care was taken to adorn the body with paint, permanent tatoos, and jewelry. A common form of jewelry was the torque—a thick, heavy, collarlike necklace. These bore symbols so intricately etched that the workmanship astonishes those who view the few examples that have been preserved, such as the beautiful Broighter Collar, housed at the National Museum of Ireland.

But the Celts' strong sense of their own individuality was both a virtue and a vice. So self-absorbed were they, as solitary members and as tribes, that they fought constantly with each other and thus were unable to mount a cohesive defense when threatened by outsiders. According to current newspapers, some of the children of the ancient Celts still have problems negotiating truces between warring factions in their midst.

The love of storytelling, poetry, and song, as well as a tendency toward contention . . . these are all part of the legacy of the Celts.

# 5

# Brehon Law

Although the ancient Celts were known for their acts of barbarism as they swept through one European nation after another, conquering and absorbing (approximately 500–300 B.C.), they were also considered a people who loved justice and equity.

Their system of law was a marvel for its time, sophisticated, complex, and judiciously administered throughout their society by their *brehons* (attorneys). Based upon a strict caste structure, which they adopted from India, the Celts' laws were clearly defined and governed every aspect of life. The brehons traveled from town to town, settling disputes, dispensing punishment, and instructing the people on the law.

Their precepts were quite fair and sensible. For instance, if one tribesman injured another, he would be required to nurse his neighbor back to health, house and feed him during his convalescence, and even pay his doctor's fees. He would also have to do the person's work, or hire someone else to do it, until he was able to resume his duties.

Women were granted rights unheard of in other ancient societies. They were allowed to seek a divorce and to own property and businesses. Also, it was considered a worse crime to murder a woman than a man. If someone killed a female, his hand and foot would be cut off, and he would then be put to death. His family would be required to pay the victim's family twenty-one cows, a vast amount in that day.

Animals were subject to the protection of the law as well as humans. By law they could not be badly beaten, overworked, or mistreated. But they also had to obey the laws. An animal who killed a human being would be executed by hanging, the same as a person.

In 1366, an English parliament was held at Kilkenny, in Ireland, and a set of laws was adopted that made a number of things illegal: the intermarriage of English and Irish, the use of the Irish language among the English, the sale of horses and even food to the Irish during times of war, and the brehon system of law. Ancient manuscripts containing the brehon precepts were hidden by Irish scholars, who wished to safeguard their heritage. Recently, some of these documents were recovered and are preserved at Trinity College and at the British Museum in London.

# 6

# Bardic Tradition

Over the centuries, when even the crudest food and simplest shelter were dear commodities for the Irish peasantry, the spoken words and the golden dreams they wove were often the only comfort afforded the bard and his audience. A poor farmer with a leaking sod roof could live in Brian Boru's shining palace at Cashel. A widow with threadbare rags for clothes could wear Queen Grania's gold- and silver-embroidered tunics and have her hair entwined with pearls.

And the conveyor of those dreams, the purveyor of enchantment, was the revered *seanchai* . . . the bard. No higher station could be attained in Irish culture than that held by those whose storytelling abilities surpassed even that of the common Irish—who could spin a fair yarn at the tip of a blue bonnet themselves.

Traveling from village to village and cottage to cottage, the seanchai provided an evening's entertainment by sharing the mystical tales of the Tuatha De Danann and their battles with the Firbolg, or the adventures of the hero Finn MacCool, the warrior queen Grania, and Brian Boru, the great "emperor" of Ireland.

Given the seat closest to the turf fire, the best hock of meat from the soup pot, and the ardent attention of his listeners, the seanchai used the magic of his words to whisk his listeners away from their humble cottage and care-filled lives to the Land of the Ever Young.

The bards of old preserved those stories and the ability to relate those tales by handing them down through the generations. According to tradition, fathers pass the gift of poetry to their daughters and the gift of storytelling to their sons.

The Emerald Isle has given birth to such literary giants as William Butler Yeats, James Joyce, George Bernard Shaw, Padraic Colum, Jonathan Swift, Oscar Wilde, and Brendan Behan. The tradition is being upheld by such contemporary playwrights and poets as Hugh Leonard, John B. Keane, Tom Coffey, John Montague, and Brian Friel.

As long as a drop of Irish blood flows in the veins of Eirinn's sons and daughters, today's world will be richer for the telling of yesterday's tales.

# 7

# Druids

Ancient Celtic society was built upon a class structure. Every man, woman, child, and even animal was placed in a rigidly defined hierarchy. And according to their rank, their responsibilities and privileges were clearly circumscribed.

At the top of this social echelon were the kings and, equal to the kings, the Druids. The Druids were the priests, scholars, teachers, historians, and guardians of all esoteric knowledge. Known for their extraordinary wisdom, they were called upon to arbitrate disputes, to negotiate with enemy kings on behalf of their leaders, and to counsel their king on matters of great national importance or daily concerns, such as the king's health or relationship with his queen.

When a king and his chief Druid disagreed on a matter, the final word was left with the Druid, as no ruler was foolish enough to go against the advice of this holy man.

The Druidic rites were mysterious and complex. The details were kept secret, guarded first by the Druid priests themselves, then by Christian monks who didn't want to immortalize pagan rituals in writing. However, we do know that those ceremonies were performed not in a temple but outdoors, usually in groves of sacred oak trees. The ancient Celtic religion attributed spiritual awareness to all living things—human, animal, and plant—and involved the worship of all the great natural forces: sun, moon, wind, and sea. It was polytheistic and held that the gods ruled every aspect of life on earth. The Druids believed in the immortality of the spirit and in reincarnation.

If the Irish of today seem a bit overly superstitious to outsiders, let it be noted that this tendency is not based on foolish ignorance or childish fantasies. The Irish have a heritage of spirituality, believing the unseen to be as valuable—maybe even more so—as that which can be perceived with the five senses. Something of the ancient Druids remains in the children of Eire, in their heightened sensitivity to the "other world" and in their respect for all living creatures. It seems there are still Druids in Ireland.

# 8

# Ringed Forts

### (300 B.C.–Eleventh Century A.D.)

From approximately 300 B.C. until the eleventh century A.D., inhabitants of Ireland constructed living areas for themselves called ringed forts. Perhaps as many as fifty thousand of these community fortresses existed, sprinkled all over the island, providing sanctuary for half a million people over the ages.

Although they came in all shapes and sizes, the typical fort was round. The residence was usually built of stone or timber and then "ringed" by a deep ditch and a wide embankment of earth, built from the soil removed by digging the trench. Sometimes more than one ring and bank were constructed, and two or three such circular gullies and mounds provided protection for those encamped inside the circle. These man-made fortifications varied from as small as six yards wide to as much as eighty-seven yards. Within the rings, the inhabitants and their livestock enjoyed a certain degree of security from those invaders, human and animal, who would attack, steal, and kill. Many of the ringed forts were situated near rivers for easy transportation and on hilltops for a viewpoint advantage.

Some of the forts had areas notched into the mounds, probably to hold watchmen. Others contained passages leading to underground chambers. Some boasted the added protection of a stone wall that surrounded the ring.

A wide variety of artifacts has been excavated from these sites: remains of the stone and timber dwellings, metal tools, glassware, and pottery.

Fortunately, many of the forts have remained undisturbed, due in part to a widely held superstition that it is exceedingly bad luck to mess with a ringed fort (or fairy fort, as some call them) or even to be inside one, especially at night. Folklore asserts that the forts are the homes of fairy spirits who will bring ill fortune on anyone who disrupts their tranquility. And while few Irish would claim to believe such tales, told by old wives with too much time on their hands, you won't find many Irishmen or women curled up in sleeping bags, spending the night in a fairy fort.

# 9

# Come to the Fair!

Since the time of the ancient Celts, the inhabitants of the Emerald Isle have gathered together in great assemblies, more recently called fairs, for the purpose of conducting business, promoting political agendas, competing in athletic competitions, and stirring up a great deal of good, old-fashioned fun.

As recently as one hundred years ago, the local fair was a vital part of Irish society, providing an opportunity for those who raised cattle, sheep, goats, pigs, horses, or fowl to buy and sell their animals. These festivals were traditionally held in the autumn, when the hard labor of the harvest was finished.

Long before daybreak, a farmer would begin his long trek to the fair. But even before he began his journey, precautions had to be taken to ensure that his trip would be safe and prosperous. Before he left his house, he would say a quick folk prayer. He would also be sure he carried something to ward off evil spirits, such as a pinch of salt, an ember from the fire, soot, or a sprig of hazel.

Once on his way, he would have to be careful to follow a few rules of the road. If he met a funeral procession, he would have to walk backward with it for three steps. When he came upon a cairn, a mound of stones marking a place where someone had died, he would need to toss yet another stone upon the pile and say a few words of blessing, for good luck.

Once he arrived at the town or village where the fair was to be held, he would find canvas-covered stalls set up along all the *boreens*, lanes off the main street. He could purchase such delectables as apples, meat pies, gooseberries, seafood, and cups of tea. Along the central thoroughfare, shops were brightly decorated with banners and displayed a wealth of merchandise.

Often the farmer would have been accompanied by his wife and children, who would enjoy a ride on a merry-go-round, whose owner-operator traveled from fair to fair with his marvelous contraption.

Despite the pleasure and distractions offered, the true purpose of the fair was economic: selling one's livestock for top price and haggling for the best bargain when purchasing someone else's cattle and pigs. To seal the deal, the buyer would spit on his own palm and slap the seller's hand. With the business done, the farmer returned home, hopefully with a heavy wallet and a light heart.

# 10

# St. Patrick

## (385–461)

The most famous Irishman of all time wasn't even born in Ireland. But, without a doubt, St. Patrick had the greatest influence of any one individual on the past, present, and future of the Emerald Isle.

St. Patrick was born in the village of Bennaven Taberniae in Britain in 385. He was the son of Calpurnius, a deacon, and grandson of Potitus, a priest (at that time, celibacy wasn't a requirement of the priesthood). The young boy worked on his father's farm until the age of sixteen, when he was captured by the Irish in a raid and taken into slavery. An Ulster farmer named Milcho bought the lad and put him to work tending sheep on the mountain of Shemish in County Antrim.

In 407, after six years of slavery, the twenty-two-year-old escaped, but the future saint was determined to return as a missionary to Ireland and convert his captors. The history of his years in Europe is vague and contradictory, but we do know that he learned some Latin and became an ordained priest. Someone, possibly St. Germanus, appointed him bishop to Ireland. Patrick returned to Ireland in 432 as an emissary of Rome.

Patrick and his company landed in Wicklow and traveled northward to the hill of Slane in the Boyne Valley. They weren't just rambling; this destination was most deliberate. Having lived among the "pagans" of Ireland, Patrick was intimately familiar with their beliefs and customs, and he knew how to stir controversy.

The Druids, the high priests of the pagan religion, were gathered in that area to celebrate Beltine, their new year. In keeping with tradition, they were about to perform a sacred fire ritual. Throughout the land, all fires were to be extinguished. Then, along with his priests, the high king would kindle the new fire from sunlight, welcoming the new year. From its site on the hill of Tara, this flame would be seen for miles.

On top of his own prominent hill, within sight of Tara, Patrick lit a fire of his own, because it was Holy Saturday, the day before Easter. His fire was in direct violation of Druidic law, and the high king and his priests were not amused.

For his rebellious act, Patrick was brought before the royal court. According to legend, it was on that occasion when he picked a shamrock and used the humble, three-leafed plant as a symbol of the Holy Trinity, illustrating how three can be one. Before he was finished presenting his case, his accusers were converted. His mission—conceived in the slave boy's heart and mind during those years of captivity—was beginning to unfold.

Many stories have been told of Patrick's legendary travels across the island, preaching and converting as he went. Patrick's success with converting the populace was due not only to his own zeal but also to the nature of the Irish people. A curious folk, it wasn't their practice to persecute those who sought to teach or preach concepts foreign to their own. Open-minded, they listened and received. This liberal attitude kept Patrick from suffering the same fate as the martyrs who had ministered to less progressive societies.

St. Patrick's light still shines on the Emerald Isle, where, fifty thousand people annually make the pilgrimage to Croagh Patrick, a mountain where it is said the saint fasted for forty days, petitioning the Lord for the right to judge the Irish on the Last Day. And Irish around the world, native and transplanted, celebrate his accomplishments on March 17, traditionally the anniversary of his death. Each year on that day, in the city streets of Dublin, Boston, and New York, you will see people of all nationalities wearing green, claiming to be Irish, and toasting their beloved St. Patrick.

# 11

# St. Bridget

## (450–523)

In a land where women have always played an important part in shaping the destiny of their people, one holy woman rises above her venerable company. St. Bridget, the female patron saint of Ireland, was born in 450, the daughter of an Irish chieftain named Dubhtach (the Dark One) of Fang, County Louth, and a Christian maidservant.

Even as a child, she was a sweet, well-intended troublemaker. Legend has it that when she was only nine years old, the king of Leinster gave her father a jewel-encrusted sword. Worried about some poor neighbors who were ill and in desperate need, the child pried the jewels from her father's new sword and made a present of them to the hungry peasants.

When her deed was uncovered, she was in terrible trouble. The king of Leinster demanded to know why she dared to deface his precious gift. She reminded him that to give to the needy was to minister to Christ, and Christ was an even higher authority than the king of Leinster. So chastised, the king withdrew his complaint.

Later, Bridget became a dairymaid-shepherdess. She is said to have performed the miracle of milking her cows three times in one day to feed hungry, unexpected guests.

The young woman was known far and wide for her extraordinary beauty but turned away the multitude of would-be suitors in favor of the church and a life as a "bride of Christ."

Bridget's nuns were known as the Guardians of the Fire of St. Bridget. Legend says that these women kept the holy fire aflame amid every sort of plunder, pillage, and hardship, constantly feeding the blaze but never generating more ash.

Numerous other miracles were associated with St. Bridget. Supposedly, the sick could be healed merely by passing through her shadow. Her cloak was also a powerful tool of healing, as desperately ill people became whole simply by touching it. According to legend, she hung her wet cloak on a ray of sunlight to dry.

Bridget died in Kildare on February 1, 523. Many kind and lovely Irish lasses bear the name of this revered saint, who seems to have handed down to her namesake "daughters" the qualities of kindness and concern for those less fortunate, as well as the great virtue of Irish hospitality.

# 12

# Ossian and Princess Niav

Part of the Irish legacy is the collection of colorful folk stories that have been handed down generation after generation for, in some cases, thousands of years. One of the most beloved stories that has survived the ages is the tale of Ossian and Princess Niav of the Golden Hair. Its setting is a place even more enchanting than Peter Pan's "Never Never Land."

Long, long ago, a young man by the name of Ossian lived in the shadow of Carrantouhill, a mountain with a strange, crooked peak, the highest point of Macgillycuddy's Reeks.

One night, he had been fishing in one of the beautiful Killarney lakes and had fallen asleep on the shore. When he woke, he looked out across the black waters of the lake, which glistened with moonlight, and spied a beautiful woman rising up from the depths of the water on a giant white steed. The woman's hair spilled around her in thick golden waves, and she wore a dress so delicate it looked as though it had been spun from moonsilver. Her stallion's trappings were made of gold and were lined with tiny silver bells that made a delightful tinkling sound with the horse's every movement.

Slowly, she rode toward Ossian. He rose, hardly daring to believe his eyes. Then she beckoned to him. "My name is Princess Niav of the Golden Hair," she said. "Come away with me." She held out her hand to him. "I'll take you to my home, Tir na nOg, the Land of the Ever Young. It is a place with no sadness, no toil or trouble, no illness or death. You will live happily there with me forever."

Ossian quickly climbed into the saddle behind her and wrapped his arms around her waist. A moment later, the horse was flying through the air. It took them far out over the lake; then, miraculously, it dived into the water and below, further and further down to an enchanted land that was everything the princess had said it would be.

Ossian lived there for a very long time. How long, he didn't know for sure, because time seemed to stop in that magic place. But as happy as he was, a longing began to ache deep in his heart: the desire to see MacGillycuddy's Reeks again, to roam the green fields of his youth, to visit his parents, brothers, and sisters.

When he told the princess of his homesickness, she warned him that going home would not be as satisfying as he hoped it would be. "You've been away for longer than you realize," she told him. "Although you haven't changed, your home has, and those you love. Stay with me and try to be content."

So Ossian stayed, but a homesick Irishman is a sorry fellow indeed, and he finally told her he must return. Sadly, she gave him the steed that had brought them to Tir na nOg, along with this warning: "Whatever you do, don't dismount from your horse. If you set foot on your native soil, you will never return to me."

Ossian gave her a kiss and a promise to return and raced away on the enchanted stallion.

The horse took him to exactly the same spot he had left, and Ossian rode around the countryside, observing all the changes that had occurred in his absence. His family home and a nearby castle now lay in terrible ruin. He met only a few people on the roads, and none of their faces were familiar to him. When he inquired about his family, no one had any knowledge or memory of them. Ossian had been away for fifteen hundred years.

Heartbroken, he decided to return to Tir na nOg and headed his horse back toward the lake. But when he reached the water, he saw an old man there, struggling to lift a heavy sack. When the elderly fellow saw Ossian, he shouted, "Would you help me with this sack?"

Ossian was a courteous lad who respected his elders, so he promptly dismounted to give assistance. But the moment his foot touched the ground, he withered, then crumbled into dust.

# 13

# Brendan the Navigator

(484–577)

The Irish have never been accused of being overly humble. We will lay claim to almost any invention, idea, victory, or achievement. So it is hardly surprising that we maintain that one of our own discovered America.

The explorer we believe accomplished this deed was a Kerryman from Clonfert called Brendan the Navigator. He was later canonized and called St. Brendan.

Brendan was born in 484, in Fenit, County Kerry. His childhood home was surrounded by water—the sea, lakes, and rivers—and the young boy received a practical education in all forms of boats and seafaring skills. From the nearby mountaintop, Brandon Hill, he could see both the Atlantic Ocean and the lakes of Killarney. And once, while praying on this mountain, he believed he caught a glimpse of Hy Brasil, or the "Isle of the Blessed, Land of the Ever Young." According to legend, this exotic land could only be seen from this spot once every seven years.

Brendan was intrigued and considered making the voyage. In that day monks often traveled far and wide to spread the Gospel, so the concept was a familiar one. Enlisting the cooperation of a few companions, Brendan set out in coracles of the type still used by Connemara fishermen—small, light vessels ribbed and sided with wood and strengthened with iron and ox hides.

Sometime between 520 and 530, Brendan and his company sailed across the Atlantic, through a foggy, cold sea of icebergs, down a long coast of an unknown land to a place of flowers and sunshine. If you believe every word of the tale, the navigator had discovered what is now Florida. They had gone only a short way inland when an angel appeared to Brendan and warned him that this was not the time to explore this new world. The heavenly host ordered him to return to Ireland, which he did.

It takes a stretch of the imagination to believe that Brendan and his men made that voyage in primitive vessels made of ox hide, wood, and iron. But it isn't completely unbelievable. Apparently, Christopher Columbus read the account of St. Brendan's journey before he set sail in 1492. And Columbus may have believed . . . at least a little.

# 14

# The Irish Language

Also called Gaelic, the Irish language was introduced to the Emerald Isle by the Celts, who arrived around 500 B.C. Irish is a cousin to Scottish Gaelic, Welsh, and Breton, all of which are Celtic languages. Complex, beautiful, and almost impossible to speak for those not exposed to it at an early age, Irish is, according to the Constitution, the national language of Ireland, while English is considered the second, even though it is far more commonly spoken on the island.

The Irish language is the oldest written vernacular in Europe and was the primary spoken language in Ireland until the 1800s. The first president of the republic, Douglas Hyde, was one of the founders of the Gaelic League, designed to keep the ancient language alive. Irish schools have taught it since 1922, preserving this important aspect of Irish culture that nearly died during the years of domination.

Having a greater, deeper understanding of the Irish language has enabled scholars to uncover more and more distinctly Irish history, that of a nation in its own right, not merely one possessed by others.

Today the Irish-speaking communities are mostly rural, located on the western seaboard, on offshore islands, in Dingle and Connemara, and also in Counties Donegal, Cork, and Waterford. These areas, known as Gaeltacht (pronounced "Gwale-tuct"), have a population of about forty thousand people who speak primarily Irish and use English only occasionally as a second language.

The Irish prime minister's title is *taoiseach* (pronounced "tee-shuck"), and the police are called the *gardai* (pronounced "guardee"). Radio and television stations around the country traditionally sign off in Irish. And most road, street, and highway signs in Ireland list the Irish name first with its English translation below. Many stores and shops display signs in Irish.

For those of you who would like to attempt a bit of the old language yourselves, wrap your tongues around this one if you can:

*Dia's Muire dhuit* (pronounced "de-a iss mu-ra guit")—which means, "God and Mary be with you."

# 15

# Ah . . . the Scent of a Turf Fire!

There is one unique, delightful scent that will stir the olfactory memory of anyone who has ever spent time in Ireland, should they catch a whiff of it on a misty evening. No, it isn't the smell of an Irish stew simmering on the back burner or even the sweet, clean fragrance of the air itself. 'Tis the indescribable redolence of a turf fire. Few sensory perceptions can induce such a cozy feeling of comfort, well-being, and hospitality.

Centuries ago, one of our great, great grandfa'rs was sitting around shivering one rainy night, listening to his missus complain of the cold. Having burned the last of their wood, he decided to toss a hunk of that black stuff from the earth onto the fire. Lo and behold, it produced a lovely, long-burning, aromatic blaze . . . and the common man in Ireland would never be cold again!

But what is turf, cut from the earth itself in brick shapes, dried, and burned on the hearths of Ireland to this day?

If there's anything as plentiful as soft, misty evenings in Ireland, it's bogs. And those bogs are filled with peat, partially carbonized vegetation that has been decomposing for ages. Using a special shovel called a slane, this peat can be cut into brick shapes, which are then allowed to dry in the sun, creating this wonderful, practical fuel called turf.

Many establishments, like pubs, bed and breakfasts, hotels, and restaurants have a turf fire going on the hearth, more to provide atmosphere than heat.

In gift shops tourists can buy small, thimble-sized bits of turf and an incense burner–type dish to take home with them. If they become homesick for the smell of Ireland on a misty evening, they can throw an Irish stew into the crock pot and light a bit of the turf, close their eyes, and invoke the spirit of "ould" Eirinn.

# 16

# St. Columba

## (521–597)

St. Columba's baptismal name was Crimthann, which means "wolf." This name might have more accurately described his personality than the gentler "Columba," which means "dove." The great "Dove of the Church" struggled all his life with his temper and arrogance. But, his faults aside, this Irish saint was primarily responsible for the conversion of the Scottish Highlands to Christianity.

Born in Garton, County Donegal, in 521, Columba was the great-grandson of Niall of the Nine Hostages, a powerful chieftain. While only a child, Columba gave his wealth to the church and became a monk. But the young man was a handful of trouble for his mentors. While visiting his former teacher, Finian of Moville, Columba was shown a precious volume that contained the Book of Psalms. Columba coveted the manuscript and asked for permission to copy it. Finian said no, but Columba defied his master's wishes and secretly duplicated it. When his "crime" was discovered, his master was furious and demanded that the copy be given to him as well. Columba refused.

Unable to resolve the problem, the two men asked the high king, Diarmait, to adjudicate the matter. Diarmait judged in favor of Finian, and Columba relinquished the manuscript.

Soon afterward, King Diarmait did something much worse in Columba's estimation. One of Columba's kinsmen, in serious trouble with the king's soldiers, sought sanctuary with Columba. Diarmait's men broke that sanctuary, seized the lad, and dragged him away to be executed. Furious, Columba raised an army among his own people to fight Diarmait.

Columba's tribe met Diarmait's on the battlefield in Culdreimhne, County Sligo, and in the course of the day's fierce fighting three thousand men died. Full of guilt for what he had done, Columba vowed he would save as many souls as he had caused to be lost that day on the battlefield.

His self-imposed penance was to be exiled from the Ireland that he loved, and he left in the year 563 at the age of forty-two. Thus began his travels throughout western and northern Scotland, preaching, converting, and establishing monasteries. It is believed the Book of Kells was written at his famous ecclesiastic monastery of Iona (see CHAPTER 18). St. Columba died at Iona in 597.

# 17

# The Golden Age of Ireland

## (400–800)

After St. Patrick's successful conversion of Ireland to the Christian faith in the early 400s, the Irish were afire with enthusiasm for their new religion. Pagan chieftains and warriors traded their swords for the simple robes of monks; queens and milkmaids became nuns; and monasteries sprang up everywhere, until nearly every community had its own monastic center for learning religion, history, and culture. Some of the ruins of those monasteries can still be found at Clonmacnoise, in Glendalough; in Ardmore; in Clonfert; and in many other locations throughout Ireland.

"Pilgrims for the Love of Christ" spread the gospel across Ireland and beyond to Europe. Saint Patrick's evangelical movement had come full circle, back to Rome.

This period, ushered in by the arrival of Christianity in Ireland, is called the Golden Age. It was a time of incredible artistic accomplishment. As the art of that period was created by newly converted pagans, the works reflect both Christian and ancient Gaelic influence, using symbolism that varies from the most sacred of Christian symbols, the cross, to intricate Celtic scrollwork, representing reincarnation and the infinite nature of the soul.

These artistic creations were wrought in metal, in the form of jewelry and sacred vessels, poetry, wood and leather work, and illuminated manuscripts. The most famous examples of these exquisitely decorated scripts are the Book of Kells, currently displayed at Trinity College in Dublin, and the Book of Durrow.

The breathtaking Ardagh Chalice, created in the mid-eighth century, shows the intricacy of Irish craftsmanship (see CHAPTER 20). About seven inches high and nine and a half inches across, the silver cup is decorated with a fine, elaborate filigree of gold bands and red and blue cloisonné enamel. The Tara Brooch was silver-gilt with gold filigree, enhanced with brilliantly colored glass and amber; it was fashioned in the early eighth century (see CHAPTER 19).

Since the Vikings, who frequently visited the monasteries, had a tendency to abscond with whatever they could carry in the way of loot, the Irish craftsmen learned to create art that was too heavy to lift, even for muscular Northmen. One answer to the problem was to carve in stone, rather than precious metal. Many of the elaborately carved stone crosses that grace the countryside were produced during the Golden Age. They bear the same combination of Celtic and Christian symbolism as the other art of the period, and some portray scenes from the Old and New Testaments.

During the Golden Age, the monastic scholars of Ireland were greatly respected by the nobility of Europe and welcomed into their courts. As well as founding churches, the monks compiled libraries of handwritten manuscripts and established schools where the information was shared with knowledge-hungry students. The monks studied Celtic history and mythology and recorded it for posterity; much of what we know of the ancient Celts comes from these annals.

So respected were the Irish scholars that foreign royalty sent their own historians, poets, theologians, and mathematicians to Ireland for educational training. The Emerald Isle was, indeed, the scholastic seat of Europe during that era.

Although Ireland was not politically unified during that period, the country did enjoy a certain sense of unity, based upon religious fervor and love of art, literature, craftsmanship, and language . . . perhaps not all that different from the Ireland of today.

# 18

# The Book of Kells

(760–820)

Simply displayed in the Long Room, the library of Trinity College in Dublin, is one of Ireland's greatest national treasures, the Book of Kells. The quintessential masterpiece of Irish manuscript illumination, a crowning achievement in the Golden Age of Irish craftsmanship, this 335-page document contains portions of the Gospels. It is thought to have been written sometime between A.D. 760 and A.D. 820. Some scholars believe it may be even older. No one has determined the original monastery where it was created or the identities of the artists, but experts believe it is the work of at least four highly skilled monks.

Although the manuscript was never completed—probably due to the invasion of the Vikings—the book remains breathtakingly beautiful. Some claim no human hand could accomplish such intricate beauty, that it must have been penned by angels. The vividly colored letters seem to have a life of their own, scrolling, winding, dissolving, and evolving into mythical, magical images of men, beasts, birds, seraphim, and devils.

The book's history illustrates the miracle of its survival to present day. Although scholars have passionately debated the history of the book for years, many believe that the treasure was penned at Iona, an island off Argyll in western Scotland, then carried from there to the church at Kells in County Meath, Ireland. The manuscript was stolen from Kells in 1007—some think during a Viking raid—stripped of its golden cover, buried, and recovered three months later. The book was then returned to Kells and kept there until 1661, when the bishop of Meath presented it to Trinity College.

Originally one large book, the manuscript was rebound in 1953 into four volumes. To protect the heavy vellum pages from fading in the sunlight, each day a fresh page is turned. The library always displays two of the four volumes. One book is turned to a completely illuminated page, while the other shows only text.

No trip to Dublin is complete without a detour to Trinity for a glimpse of this beautiful bit of Irish history. Having endured century after century of war, marauding, pillage, and plunder, the Book of Kells remains a silent but powerful testament to the artistry of the Irish soul. Or, as James Joyce called it, "the fountainhead of Irish inspiration."

# 19

# The Tara Brooch

## (Eighth Century)

The eighth-century Tara Brooch is a radiant example of the high level of craftsmanship achieved by artisans during Ireland's Golden Age (c. 400–c. 800) and continues to be a source of great national pride.

Personal decoration was an important form of expression for the ancient Celts. Among their most prized personal possessions were the brooches they used to pin their cloaks at the shoulder. Peasants wore simple ones made of iron, while nobles sported beautiful works of art, wrought with gold, silver, and precious gemstones.

By the eighth century, the creation of these ornaments had developed into an intricate and complex art form among Irish metalsmiths. And, although other simpler, less impressive artifacts have been uncovered, the Tara Brooch is the finest example that has been found and preserved to date.

The extremely high quality of workmanship and the value of the materials used indicate that the Tara Brooch was crafted for a woman of high social standing and wealth, probably the wife of a chieftain, brehon, or bard.

The brooch, made of cast silver-gilt, is beautifully ornamented with gold filigree panels and decorated with colored glass and pieces of amber. The designs on the piece, similar to the intricate symbols and scrollwork found in illuminated manuscripts such as the Book of Kells, include animals, birds, and unidentifiable, mythical creatures, as well as abstract Celtic curlicues—only these were worked in metal and with gems rather than in ink.

The brooch bears gratuitous decoration on the back that can only be seen by the person as she pins it on her garment; similarly, the Ardagh Chalice has ornate decorations on the bottom to be viewed only by the priest who used it (see CHAPTER 20). Clearly, the artist was creating for the pleasure of art, aside from practicality.

Of all the metalwork done in the Golden Age, the Tara Brooch is one of the finest testimonies to the combination of man-developed skill and God-given talent so highly valued at that time in the Irish culture.

The Tara Brooch is presently housed in the National Museum of Ireland in Dublin.

# 20

# The Ardagh Chalice

## (Eighth Century)

In 1868, a Mr. Quin of Ardagh made a marvelous discovery. While engaged in the humble occupation of digging potatoes in an old fort on his land, he unearthed the Ardagh Chalice. This chalice, wrought during Ireland's golden Age, is an exquisite example of Irish artistry at its finest, a tangible representation of the spiritual transition of a people. Crafted during the eighth century by a highly skilled but unknown metalsmith, the design of the chalice shows the influence of both pagan religion and Christianity.

When Ireland converted to Christianity, many of the chieftains became priests, while retaining much of their ancient symbolism in their art. The interlocking scrollwork that typifies pagan Celtic design represents the infinite nature of the soul, reincarnation and renewal, the ever-repeating patterns of life and death. The creatures depicted in the art of this period represent man and beast, virtual and mythical, pagan and Christian.

The chalice stands seven inches high and is nine and a half inches in diameter. The cup is attached by a stem to a conical base. The plain silver surface complements the elaborate gold bands and panels with red and blue cloisonné enamel bosses. The delicate gold filigree and colored enamelwork make this chalice a rare beauty to behold. The cup is decorated with the spirals and Celtic-style animals mentioned earlier, even on the bottom, although this would be seen only by a priest raising the chalice for consecration.

No doubt sensing the significance of his find, Mr. Quin asked that the cup be examined by Lord Dunraven and Bishop Butler of Limerick. Intrigued and excited, they passed it on to the Royal Irish Academy, which verified its antiquity and importance as a great archeological treasure.

Bishop Butler bought the chalice from Mr. Quin on June 21, 1871, and the cup was presented to the Royal Irish Academy in 1878.

The Ardagh Chalice, an expression of the creativity and skill of the Irish people, is now at home in the National Museum in Dublin.

# 21

# Round Towers

## (Mid-Eighth Century)

One of the most interesting and charming examples of Irish architecture is the round tower. Across the island, these stone sentinels bear silent witness to a more violent age, the mid-eighth century, when these structures were built to provide refuge from murderous raids.

It didn't take long for the Norsemen to discover that the Irish monasteries provided a treasure trove for marauding invaders. Guarded only by monks, who were primarily scholars, not warriors, the monastic settlements contained a wealth of gold and jewels in the form of sacred vessels, manuscripts covers, and other precious art objects. Easy pickings for the Vikings, the monasteries were constantly attacked; their precious possessions were stolen and, often, their priests slaughtered.

A partial solution was found in the form of the round tower. These one-hundred-foot structures served a triple purpose: a watchtower, from which the approaching invaders could be seen from afar and the populace alerted; a bell tower, to announce times of prayer, to sound alarms, etc.; and most important, a place of refuge. The door to the tower was placed at an inconvenient, but sensible, sixteen or so feet from the ground and was accessible only by ladder—a ladder that was then drawn up and in once the priests and their treasures were safely inside. The towers were practical,

to be sure, but they were also structures of beauty, graceful symbols of sanctuary.

Over one hundred towers remain in Ireland, though most are little more than ruins. But a few are still intact. Those that are standing, noble reminders of ages gone by, include the fine examples at Glendalough in County Wicklow, Nendrum in County Down, and Devenish in County Fermanaugh.

# 22

# Brian Boru, Emperor of the Irish
### (926–1014)

Called the emperor of Ireland, the great high king Brian Boru was the only man ever to unite the whole island of Eire under one leader.

Born in 926, Brian MacCennedi was named king of the Dal Cais clan of Munster, when his older brother was murdered in 976. Tall, well-educated in battle tactics, strong of body, personality, and character, Brian came from excellent leadership stock. He quickly pursued the kingship of all Munster, with the ultimate goal of becoming high king of Ireland.

Brian wasn't content to be high king in name only, like his predecessors. At that time, the office was so loosely defined, the support from tribal chieftains so unpredictable, that the title meant little. Ireland desperately needed strong leadership. Under siege from the Vikings, the Irish had to make a united stand or continue to suffer their pillage and plunder.

Brian's goal became a burning mission when the high king of that time, Mael Sechnaill II, threatened by Brian's growing strength, attacked the Dal Cais in their homeland. Enraged, Brian led retaliatory attacks against Mael Sechnaill.

The battle continued for years until, in 1002, Mael Sechnaill surrendered the title to Brian. But being the emperor of the Irish was a difficult task for any man, let alone one who was seventy-six years old. Brian worked hard, coaxing and coercing the allegiance of the lesser kings, suppressing revolts, collecting tribute, protecting and rebuilding monasteries and schools, and, of course, fighting the Vikings. He also found time to play the harp and compose songs and poems.

Toward the end of his reign, old problems with the northern kings began to resurface, and the Vikings in Dublin decided to resume their favorite pastimes, murder and mayhem.

Brian and Mael Sechnaill had a parting of the ways, and Mael Sechnaill withdrew his military support from Brian just before a planned battle with the Vikings. In spite of the defection, Brian felt he had enough troops to proceed, so they assembled at Clontarf near the sea in Dublin Bay. On April 23, 1014, Good Friday, the final battle between Brian Boru and the Vikings began.

At the age of eighty-eight, Brian was too old to take command of the bloody hand-to-hand combat, so he watched from the sidelines as his son Murchad led the fight. The Irish won, but paid a terrible price:

Brian's son Murchad was killed, as well as three of the Viking nobles. Brian himself was felled by the axe of a fleeing Viking who found the old king's tent unguarded. Brian's body was carried from the battlefield and buried with great ceremony in Armagh. One of the survivors of Clontarf, a Viking, recorded the outcome in his own words: "Brian fell, but won at last."

# 23

# The Rock of Cashel

As the song says, it's a long way to Tipperary, but if it's the rock of Cashel you've come to see, the journey is more than worth the effort. Rising three hundred feet above the Tipperary plain in central Ireland, the Rock of Cashel has been called the Acropolis of Ireland. A magnificent sight from near or far, the Rock of Cashel appears to be an enormous castle when viewed from a distance.

Actually, it is a combination of ruins, structures known as the Hall of the Vicar's Chorale, Cormac's Chapel, and the Cathedral. At the base of the rock stands the Dominican Friary, part of which dates back to the fifteenth century; another section was built as early as the thirteenth century. Most prominent among the buildings is the incredible Round Tower, ninety-two feet tall with a door twelve feet above the ground. The tower is sandstone and topped with an unusual conical cap.

"Cashel" comes from the Gaelic *caiseal,* meaning "stone fort." For centuries considered a sacred site, the ancient Celts worshiped atop the rock, Irish chieftains built castles on it, and kings were crowned there. For seven centuries it was the seat of the kings of Munster.

At the Rock is a treasure, Saint Patrick's Cross. A beautiful and unusual type of stone cross, it is the base of the monument that is reputed to be the coronation stone of the kings of Munster. It is also where Brian Boru was crowned (see CHAPTER 22).

The Rock of Cashel has an almost magical presence about it—a surreal, mystical quality. Standing there, watching the clouds race over the emerald-and-gold checkered plains of Tipperary spread below you, you can feel a chill shiver over your skin that has nothing to do with the cool, damp morning fog.

Over the centuries, Irish kings lived on that very spot, enjoying daily life with their families. Generation after generation died there— some from illness, some from old age, and many from fierce battles with enemies or family and friends who betrayed them.

The Rock seems to have absorbed it all: the joy, the sadness, the terror, the rage, but most of all that deep, gracious, quiet understanding that comes only from time.

# 24

# Grania
## (1530–1583)

Grace O'Malley, better known as Grania, was a tough lady. This swashbuckling queen of a shipping and piracy empire off the coast of Galway reigned at the same time as Elizabeth I of England, first her nemesis, later her ally. Invited to attend Elizabeth's court, Grania was offered the title of countess, which she refused. When an English fleet was sent to destroy her, Grace fortified herself and her people in Carrigahooly Castle, the home of her husband.

Grace was born in County Mayo around 1530. A tall woman, she had a swarthy complexion, black hair, and dark eyes. She had two husbands, the first being Donal O'Flaherty, lord of Ballynahinch and king of Connemara, who died in a sea battle. Grace's career in piracy began innocently enough as the fourteen-year-old aided her husband in his smuggling trade. She graduated to having her own raiding vessels, manned by thirty rowers and another fifty or more warriors. Based on Clare Island, they preyed on English merchant vessels and Spanish galleons.

Grania's second husband was Sir Richard Burke, a member of a powerful Anglo-Norman family. The marriage was a practical one. Because of the strategic position of his castle, Rockfleet, Grania would have control of Clew Bay, a busy, prosperous harbor. On her side, Grania brought to the union much wealth, power, and prestige—along with fighting men, a particular attraction for a man whom Irish historians described as an "unquiet and rebellious man" who was always feuding with his neighbors.

Much of the history we have of Grace O'Malley comes from the state papers of Elizabeth I, where the pirate queen's exploits are recorded. One of Elizabeth's viceroys called Grania "a most famous feminine sea-captain." A less complimentary Englishman claimed she was "a nurse of all rebellions in Connaught" (the northwestern province of Ireland).

The last ten years of Grace's life were spent in relative peace at her beloved Rockfleet, overlooking the beautiful and dramatic Clew Harbor. She died there of a lingering illness in 1603 (the same year Elizabeth I died). They say she is buried on Clare Island in Clew Bay in the small island's abbey church.

# PART II

# Ireland's Joys
# and Woes

# 25

# Jonathan Swift

(1667–1745)

Most of the world knows Jonathan Swift as the author of the delightful children's tale *Gulliver's Travels*. But the Irish are proud of Swift because he is one of the most brilliant satirists in literary history. He wrote some of the grimmest indictments of British oppression of Ireland ever penned. Even, *Gulliver's Travels* (1726), his fanciful story of a giant in the land of diminutive Lilliputians, is underwritten with complex subtext concerning the failings of mankind.

Swift was born in Ireland on November 30, 1667, one of six sons of a British clergyman. He received the finest education the English aristocracy in Ireland could provide, including a four-year degree from Trinity College, Dublin. But Swift hated Ireland, which he called "the most miserable country upon earth." Despite his Irish birth, Swift considered himself English, not one of the "savage old Irish," as he described the natives. In the midst of political unrest following the Revolution of 1688, he departed Ireland for England.

While in England, Swift didn't receive the sort of recognition he believed he deserved. In 1694, he reluctantly returned to Ireland, where he was ordained an Anglican priest.

Again, he left Ireland for England, where he pursued his life's ambition, a bishopric on English soil. Instead, in 1714, at the age of forty-seven, he was awarded the prestigious position of dean of St. Patrick's . . . back in Ireland. With a heavy heart he returned home, where he faithfully served as St. Patrick's dean for the next seven years. Walking daily from his home to St. Patrick's, he passed through some of Dublin's worst slums, which were overrun with out-of-work weavers and craftsmen.

In 1720, the economic oppression of the Irish by the English motivated Swift to write a highly controversial pamphlet, *A Proposal for the Universal Use of Irish Manufacture.* Publishing it anonymously, he encouraged the Irish to buy everything Irish and "burn everything from England except her coal."

In March 1724, Swift penned the *Drapier's Letters,* which denounced the decision made by Charles II concerning the minting of Irish coins outside of Ireland. The issue wasn't really who was going to mint the 'ha'penny. It was about Ireland having its own mint. It was about freedom. Once again, the government wanted to prosecute the writer. But although everyone knew that Swift was the infamous drapier, it couldn't be proven, as no one would offer evidence against him.

Between 1727 and 1730, Ireland suffered a famine. The bodies of the dead and dying lay openly in the streets, and as it had many times before, the government did far too little, too late. Horrified, Swift wrote a shockingly bitter pamphlet called *A Modest Proposal for Preventing the Children of Poor People in Ireland From Being a Burden to Their Parents or the Country.* In this tract, published in 1729, he suggested that "one-fourth part of the infants under two years old be forthwith fattened as dainty bits for landlords, who, as they have already devoured most of the parents, seem to have best right to eat up the children."

For his efforts on their behalf, the Irish considered Swift a patriot— even though he criticized them, too, in his writings, holding them partially responsible for their own miseries because of their complacency and defeatism. The Irish embrace those who speak truth, complimentary or not.

Sadly, on August 17, 1745, the seventy-four-year-old Swift was declared "of unsound mind and memory." In a poem he said of himself, "He gave the little Wealth he had, to build a House for Fools and Mad." On October 19, 1745, Swift died and left the greater part of his estate to build a hospital for the mentally ill.

# 26

# Irish Curses

Anyone might utter a curse after splashing coffee down the front of his favorite shirt or dropping something heavy on her left foot, but to the Irish people cursing is a serious business. And at the risk of sounding less than humble, we're better at it than most.

Throughout a history of oppression, a deftly articulated curse was often the only recourse available to the poor. A woman whose husband was hanged for looking cross-eyed at a landowner might be heard to mutter at the foot of her mate's gallows, "May the Devil cut the heads off all landlords, and may he make a day's work of their necks." Or a lowly peasant, ousted from his humble cottage, might proclaim of his landlord's agent, "May the Devil swallow him sideways and choke on his pecker."

This is not to say that the Irish blithely curse whomever crosses their path. It's one thing to say to someone who's proving a nuisance, "It's a briar on the seat of me britches you are. Wherever I go, it's you behind me." But it's quite another to send someone "to hell, with never a drop o' Guinness to quench your eternal thirst."

Every Irishman and Irish woman knows that an ill-aimed curse directed at an innocent party will "come home to roost like Bridget's hens," bringing the curser more misery than he or she had already. So maledictions are judiciously dispensed, and the honest person needn't be afraid of receiving one.

But if it happens that a poor widow woman fixes you with a baleful eye, turn tail and run as though the Old Horned One himself had set fire to your backside. Because if you dally, you might hear this potent condemnation: "May he be afflicted with the rot; may the worms take his eyes and the crows pluck out his entrails; but may he stay alive until we're all sick of the sight of him."

# 27

# James Hoban

## (1762–1831)

The Executive Mansion in Washington, D.C., is one of the most beautiful and regal residences in the world, home of the president of the United States of America. More commonly known as the White House, it is the symbol of the highest office of the land, stately, elegant, and imposing. And it was designed by the Irish architect James Hoban, who also worked on the design and building of the U.S. Capitol.

Hoban is believed to have been born in County Kilkenny, Ireland, in 1762 and was educated at the University of Dublin. He emigrated to the United States in 1785, settling in Charleston, South Carolina, where he established himself as a respected architect. In 1792 he relocated to Washington, where he designed and directed the building of the neoclassical Executive Mansion. During the War of 1812, enemy British forces burned the mansion, and Hoban rebuilt it, improving upon his original design.

# 28

# Irish Blessings

You haven't received a true and proper benediction until a person of Irish descent bids a ray of sunlight from heaven to shine upon your head.

Accused of being naively superstitious, the Irish believe that great power lies in words, that something good or bad can be literally "spoken" into being. Therefore, when a blessing is bestowed upon you by one of Eirinn's sons or daughters, you can be assured that it was given with the most heartfelt wishes for your well-being.

Some of these traditional blessings might involve the health of your physical body, the destination of your immortal soul, and even the weight of your wallet. Some are meant to smooth the rocky road of romance, and some of the more poignant express the desire of everyone sprouted from an Irish family tree: that you might live your days, every last one of them, on Irish soil.

Those who have had to leave that verdant land—or whose foreparents were forced aboard emigrant ships by starvation, deprivation, or deportation, bound for another place, not so green, not so magical—can take comfort in knowing "home" is only an Irish blessing away.

So if you feel the need or even a gentle desire to call a bit of heaven into someone's life, here are some traditional blessings . . . tried and true:

> May the good Lord hold you in the hollow of His hand, and may He not close his fist too tightly on you.
>
> May I see you with a silver head and combing your grandchildren's hair.
>
> When you look at the world through the bottom of a glass, may you see someone ready to buy.
>
> Here's to absent friends, and here's twice to absent enemies.
>
> May the doctor never earn a pound out of you.
>
> May the frost never afflict your spuds.

# 29

# Turlough O'Carolan
## (1670–1738)

Turlough O'Carolan claimed, "I spent a time in Ireland happy and contented, drinking with every strong man who was a real lover of music." In a land as passionate about its music as Ireland, O'Carolan must have consumed a great deal of drink, while being extraordinarily happy and contented. Only a land of music lovers could have spawned this man, the latest and greatest of Irish bards, Turlough O'Carolan.

The last of the wonderful harpist-composers lived from 1670 to 1738 and hailed from the village of Newtown, County Meath. Although he was blinded by smallpox at the age of fourteen, he traveled far and wide, entertaining and composing. His services were hired by the landed gentry of the day, who supplied the musician with fresh horses for his journeys, as well as a servant to carry his harp.

Under at least one circumstance, O'Carolan credited the "good people" with inspiring some of his melodies. He said he spent the night in a fairy fort (see CHAPTER 8), and claimed that upon awakening, his head was filled with their haunting tunes.

On March 25, 1738, O'Carolan died as the result of a lingering illness at the age of sixty-eight. He was buried in the ancient cemetery of Kilronan on the shores of Lough Meelagh.

In the twentieth century, O'Carolan's music was rediscovered and revived by contemporary artists like Sean O'Riada. Americans owe O'Carolan a special debt of gratitude; he wrote the music to which the stirring lyrics of Francis Scott Key were set, creating the national anthem, "The Star-Spangled Banner." Sadly, due to widely accepted misinformation, another fellow generally has been credited with that accomplishment.

# 30

# Hedgerow Schools
(1691–1831)

In 1691, the Irish Protestant parliament in Dublin passed a set of decrees called the Penal Laws, which—short of outlawing Catholicism altogether—made life as difficult as possible for the Irish Catholics. Excluding Catholics from holding office, carrying weapons, intermarrying with Protestants, and bequeathing their land to any Catholic relative, the laws almost made it illegal for children to receive any education other than one espousing Protestantism.

The Irish scholars, many of them persecuted priests, came to the fore, risking their freedom, even their lives, to teach the children of Ireland. They organized hedgerow schools, so named because they were held in secret places, hidden from the prying eyes of the authorities, often behind the lowly hedges and in barns during inclement weather.

The Irish people have always placed tremendous value upon education. And, although their surroundings were humble, they taught such subjects as Irish, English, Latin, Greek, geography, and arithmetic.

The hedgerow master was held in high esteem among the families of his students; his was almost as lofty a position as the parish priest's. He was invited to all social functions, and his advice was often solicited, especially in regard to the writing of legal documents such as leases, loan papers, petitions, and wills.

If the common Irish folk loved him, however, he was loathed by the British. When the British established a national system of schools in 1831, the hedgerow schools began to decline. But their existence provided evidence of the Irish people's love for knowledge, their passion for history, and their determination to share those gifts with their children, no matter the cost.

# 31

# The Gentle People

The Irish have been accused of being superstitious, naive, even childlike in their belief in the "Wee People." In fact, that phrase is more American than Irish. In the "auld" country, those spiritual beings who live on our periphery, usually, but not always, just out of sight, are called *daoine maithe*, which in English means "the Good People." This title may be

more of an appeasement than a description, because the Good People demand respect. Folks who don't display the proper amount of deference might find themselves victims of a bit of fairy mischief or worse.

A plethora of spiritual creatures inhabit the Emerald Isle. The *Clob-*

*hair-ceann* (pronounced "Clur-i-caun") is a fairy fellow whose favorite pastime is stealing wine from gentlemen's cellars. The *Fear Dearg* (pronounced "Far Darrig"), also known as the Red Man because of his red cap and coat, likes to play practical jokes on humans. The *Fear Gorta* or Man of Hunger is a skeletal figure who roams the land in times of famine, begging for a bit of bread and rewarding those who befriend him. The *Pooka* is a spirit who often assumes the form of an animal, one of his favorites being that of a large black dog. The *Leanhaun Shee*, which means "fairy mistress," craves love from mortals. She is the inspiration of Gaelic poets and the reason for their early deaths as she drains the life from them, even as she inspires their poetry.

Besides these land spirits, there are spirits who inhabit the waters, known as the *Moruadh* or, in English, the Merrow. The females, also known as mermaids, are beautiful and constantly trying to lure attractive human men into the sea.

Certainly the favorite is the Leprechaun, the industrious shoemaker. Since fairy folk spend most of their days and nights feasting, making love, and dancing, they frequently wear out their delicate slippers, so the Leprechaun is a busy fellow . . . and rich to boot. We all know that a Leprechaun stores his gold in a pot at the elusive end of the rainbow. If you can catch this wily fellow, he will give you his treasure in exchange for his freedom. But if you see one, don't let him out of your sight. He can disappear in the wink of a pretty lass's eye.

# 32

# (Theobald) Wolfe Tone
## (1763–1798)

Irish history is positively brimming with political heroes who died in the cause of attaining freedom for Ireland. They are all worthy of our admiration and pride, but in the company of such paladins, Wolfe Tone stands a head taller. He has been given the honorable title "father of Irish nationalism."

Born in Dublin on June 20, 1763, Wolfe Tone was the son of a well-to-do coachbuilder. He harbored dreams of a military career, but his father insisted that he attend Trinity College.

In 1791, Tone formed the Society of United Irishmen, a group fighting for parliamentary reform. The United Irishmen were particularly interested in the developments of the revolution in France, thinking they might model a rebellion of their own in Ireland after that of their French counterparts.

Part of their plans depended on gaining French support, and Tone was selected to be the one to ask for that assistance. But British authorities uncovered some papers that documented Tone's correspondence soliciting help from the French—a blatant act of treason. Rather than wait to be arrested, Tone escaped to America with his family.

He settled in Princeton, New Jersey, and had just begun to enjoy his life as a farmer when the United Irishmen again asked him to travel to France to continue the supplication on Ireland's behalf. Though he spoke hardly any French, he succeeded in persuading the French to launch an expedition on behalf of the Irish. They assembled a huge fleet armed with fifteen thousand soldiers and sailed for Ireland in December 1796 with Tone aboard. But the mission was doomed; they were unable even to land because of a hurricane. Eventually, Tone was captured by the British, tried, and condemned to be hanged, although he asked for the more dignified soldier's execution of being shot.

On November 19, 1798, Tone was found in his cell with his throat cut, still alive but in great agony. He had attempted suicide using a penknife and severed his windpipe instead of his jugular. Tone overheard a physician saying that if he were to move or try to speak, he would surely die. Tone whispered, "I can yet find word to thank you, sir. It is the most welcome news you could give me. . . . I find I am but a bad anatomist." Moments later, he died. He was only thirty-five years old.

# 33

# Robert Emmet
(1778–1803)

Freedom fighters are usually known for their deeds, but most of Robert Emmet's efforts on behalf of Irish independence had disappointing, even disastrous, results. It was his words, spoken before his execution, that would provide him a hero's place in Irish history. His final statement would inspire patriots for generations, until the dream of an Irish republic became a reality.

Robert Emmet was born in Dublin in 1778. His brother, Thomas Addis Emmet, was a well-known doctor and barrister. Thomas Emmet belonged to the United Irishmen, the pro-republic revolutionary group, and frequently defended its members who were brought to trial. His political views and fervor were passed on to his younger brother, Robert, who also joined the United Irishmen. In February 1798, the twenty-year-old Robert was attending Trinity College in Dublin, but he was forced to abandon his studies because of his political affiliations and flee the country.

He escaped to Paris, where he met other United Irishmen who had preceded him. In 1802, Thomas joined him. At that time, Napoleon appeared to be interested in launching an attack on Britain. This news was most encouraging to the United Irishmen. Having received a generous inheritance, Robert returned to Dublin and began to stockpile weapons.

When war did erupt between France and England, the United Irishmen decided to seize the opportunity. Robert began to implement his plans for a rising. But he wasn't expecting the catastrophe that would alter his scheme: an explosion at his ammunition factory. Because of this complication, the August date of the rising was moved forward to July. This caused a problem in communication and, subsequently, coordination with his compatriots, Michael Dwyer in Wicklow and Thomas Russell of Ulster. As a result, fewer than one hundred men turned out for the event, not nearly enough for the planned assault on Dublin Castle. Unfortunately, they were joined by a rowdy horde who in the end accosted a gentleman, Lord Kilwarden, and his nephew, the Rev. Mr. Wolfe, on Thomas Street and murdered them there.

Robert Emmet's glorious "rising" had been a complete disaster.

For his own safety, he should have left Dublin immediately, but he refused to go before seeing his fiancée, a young lady named Sara

Curran. Sara's father, John Philpot Curran, hated him; whether that has anything to do with what happened, we don't know, but Robert was arrested, tried, and convicted of the murders.

Emmet achieved immortality with his eloquent, stirring speech delivered from the dock:

"Let no man write my epitaph; for as no man who knows my motives dare now vindicate them, let not prejudice and ignorance asperse them. Let them and me rest in obscurity and peace; and my tomb remain uninscribed and my memory in oblivion until other times and other men can do justice to my character. When my country takes her place among the nations of the earth, then and not till then, let my epitaph be written. I have done."

He was executed on September 20, 1803, at the age of twenty-five. His words were eerily prophetic. There is no epitaph. Robert Emmet's gravesite is unknown.

## 34

# The Irish "Wise Person"

Ireland has been blessed with more than her share of individuals known from ancient times as "wise persons." Wise persons could be of either gender, but they had to be aged . . . or at least old enough to have accumulated a great deal of life experience. Also, they had to demonstrate some proof of special abilities, like the gift of prophecy or unexplained knowledge. Nowadays, such a person might be known as a psychic, but the description "wise person" includes much more.

The wise person was held in extremely high esteem in his or her village or town, and their advice and assistance was sought in times of trouble. Wise persons were especially knowledgeable about fairies—how to appease them or simply avoid them. Their esoteric wisdom also included ways of breaking an evil curse that had been put upon you and of summoning a blessing.

Wise persons were particularly adept at creating *pishogues,* which could be described as charms or incantations, that were usually designed to secure cures for people or animals. Pishogues could also protect against evil forces, bad luck, or witchcraft, increase wealth or agricultural production, and cause the object of your affections to love you. They could even throw an illness or bad luck toward your enemy.

Pishogues have fallen out of fashion in all but the most rural areas of Ireland. Now, if we want to get even, we take our neighbor to court. If we're looking for romance, we might go online with a computer service. If we want to protect ourselves from misfortune, we might take out an extra insurance policy.

The wise persons' methods were more colorful than modern ways, and whether their techniques worked or not, they gave us the illusion of control over our surroundings. Both they and their craft are sorely missed.

# 35

# Biddy Early
## (1799–1874)

Ireland's most famous "wise woman," Biddy Early, was born in the Faha Mountains of County Clare in 1799. According to folklore a "wise person" possessed special powers that could heal the sick, foresee the future, and cleanse people of curses placed on them. Biddy Early was said to be able to do all these things and more. From her home on Kilbarron Lake, she dispensed her own brand of homespun wisdom and potions.

Her powers, it is said, came from a small bottle that was either blue, black, or green. No one seems to have known for certain. But what they did know for sure was that Biddy was most effective at what she did. So good was she that she received copious gifts from grateful customers and patients, usually in the form of an alcoholic beverage. These presents were both a blessing and a curse—a curse because three of her husbands died of excessive drinking, trying to consume the bounty.

The clergy was less enamored by Biddy and opposed her constantly. She didn't allow their complaints to interfere with her business at hand, using her special gifts to help her fellow men, women, children, and beasts as well.

She was once consulted by the Prince of Wales, but in keeping with the honorable tradition of healers, she never revealed the nature of his complaint.

Although she was badly crippled in her old age, they say she made it to the lake and tossed in her precious bottle just before her death in 1874.

# 36

# Thatched Cottages

Countless travel brochures and coffee-table books about Ireland bear quaint Irish cottages on their covers. Not only are they charming, but they also bear testimony to the resourceful nature of the Irish.

Picking just the right spot to build was always a vexing problem. Not only did the location need to be practical—fairly level, not too many stones in the ground, ready access to water, and reasonably dry—but there were spiritual considerations too. Great care had to be taken not to build a cottage over a gravesite, out of respect for the dead and the fear of arousing those who should be resting peacefully. A wise fellow would also refrain from building on an area that had been a dwelling of ancient peoples.

To complicate the matter, graves and ancient dwelling sites weren't easy to detect once time had smoothed away the evidence. So the Irish had a way to "ask permission" of the spirits before they began to build. They thrust four rods into the ground, one at each corner of their proposed construction. After being left overnight, the markers were examined to see if the Good People had tampered with them. If all were still in place undisturbed, the builder could proceed with confidence.

Most of the cottages had thick, sturdy walls made of stones, usually mortared with a mixture of sand and lime or clay and lime. However, in some areas, mainly on the west coast, neither clay nor lime was attainable, so the amazing art of building "dry walls" was perfected—fitting the stones so tightly that mortar was unnecessary.

The lack of timber has been a problem in Ireland since the sixteenth and seventeenth centuries, when many of the island's forests were leveled for wood to build England's navy. Many Irish cottages had to be constructed smaller, simply because no long beams were available to support a larger roof.

A more prosperous farmer might have plenty of wheat and oats to create the warm, thatched straw roof, while a landless laborer might have to use rushes. In areas with quarries, one could have a slate roof, which was more durable than thatch but not nearly so warm. The result of using these natural materials from the immediate area was a charming cottage that blended beautifully with its surroundings, a graceful complement to the landscape.

# 37

# Hearth and Home

*No man ever wore a scarf as warm as his children's arms
around his neck.* —An old Irish proverb

If there was ever a people who loved hearth and home above all else, it is the Irish. They consider the greatest joys of life to be love of God and family, flocks of children underfoot, good company (which includes witty conversation, lively debate, and good drink), a sense of honor, and a good reputation.

If you are an honest person, lacking in hypocrisy, and don't put on airs (which they quickly detect and heartily despise), you can easily make a friend of an Irish person. And once a friend, you are part of their extended family.

And what large families they have. In most societies, any couple who has more than four or five children might be told, "It's time you two figured out what was causing that and put a stop to it!" But in Ireland, it's truly a case of "the more the merrier!" Irishmen with ten children or more will give you an account of their offspring with great pride.

At times when material goods were few and presents difficult to come by, the blessed gift of a child was the only thing a man and woman could give one another. And it was that tie which bonded a couple together during the tough times.

Whether the children are running through the house shrieking with glee or sleeping peacefully in their beds, whether the house is filled with old friends sharing a drink at the kitchen table and talking politics or only the family is within doors, the Irish heart is at home near its own hearth. As the proverb says, "There's no fireside like your own fireside."

> Three best things to have a surplus of:
>     Money after paying the rent,
>     Seed after spring,
>     And friends at home.
> —An old Irish triad

# 38

# Shamrocks

Ever since St. Patrick used the three-leafed shamrock to explain the mystery of the Holy Trinity (showing that the Father, the Son, and the Holy Spirit could be separate, but complete, parts of a whole) that humble plant has been near and dear to the hearts of the Irish. The actual species of that original shamrock has long been debated, but the most likely candidates are white clover, black medic, the wood sorrel, hop clover, and watercress.

Although a harp is the official emblem of the Emerald Isle, certainly the shamrock is the Irish symbol best known worldwide. The Irish haven't always been afforded the luxury of wearing that sign of Irish patriotism. Once it was a capital crime to wear a shamrock on St. Patrick's Day. As the words of the famous song "The Wearin' o' the Green" go:

O Paddy dear, an' did ye hear the news that's goin' round?
The shamrock is by law forbid to grow in Irish ground!
... She's [Ireland is] the most distressful country that ever yet was seen,
For they're hangin' men and women there for wearin' o' the green!

Now we can all proudly don that color in the form of a shamrock, and on St. Patrick's Day the simple shamrock is everywhere, decorating everything from doors and windows to people. In fact, according to tradition, if you aren't sporting a bit of green on St. Patrick's Day, you might be pinched by someone who is.

# 39

# Daniel O'Connell

## (1775–1847)

On January 1, 1801, the Act of Union was passed, legislating a union between Ireland and England. The Irish parliament of Dublin was resolved, the government of Ireland was transferred to the English parliament, and Ireland lost even the illusion of independence from Great Britain.

Many considered this "union" more of a forcible rape. One of those who bitterly opposed the act was a young, bold, talented attorney, Daniel O'Connell. Born on August 6, 1775, in Cahirciveen into a well-to-do, landed Kerry family, O'Connell was educated in France, studied law in London, and was called to the Irish bar in 1798.

In a speech to a group of Protestants, O'Connell declared, "Union is a crime to begin with and must continue to be, unless crime, like wine, improves with age."

O'Connell set his law practice aside and applied all his efforts toward having the Act of Union repealed and gaining Catholic emancipation. He held a mass meeting at Tara in County Meath to rally for the cause. The crowd was estimated to be half a million.

Afterward, he organized assemblies, with similar enthusiastic responses from the people who thronged to hear him. Upon seeing the multitudes who turned out to lend their support, the English became concerned about this "man of the people." When they heard that he was organizing an even larger meeting in Clontarf, they dispatched warships and troops to the area.

Afraid that violence would erupt, O'Connell sent his supporters home, saying, "Human blood is no cement for the temple of liberty." But this wasn't enough to allay the fears of the British; a week later he was arrested, convicted of conspiracy, and imprisoned. O'Connell received a light sentence of one year, but the nation was outraged. When it was confirmed that the prosecution had tampered with the jury selection, his conviction was overthrown. He was released and received a hero's welcome home, escorted by two hundred thousand ardent followers to his house in Dublin. But some of the fire had dimmed in O'Connell. He began to take a more moderate stance, believing that gaining some ground was better than losing it all.

His health broken, his heart heavy, O'Connell died on May 15, 1847, in Genoa, exiled from his beloved Ireland.

# 40

# The Great Hunger

## (1845–1848)

The potato famine of the 1840s (or the Great Hunger, as it is called by the people of Ireland) may seem an unlikely reason for those of Irish heritage to be proud. But the fact that they survived such a horrific tragedy, and emerged with their spirits scarred but intact, confirms the strength of the Irish people.

Many of us have little knowledge of the event and no comprehension of the grim truth, which is that two and a half million people died horribly and needlessly. Without knowing more about this dark period, one cannot possibly understand Ireland's troubled past or its complicated present.

By the mid-1800s, thanks to the hated Penal Laws, Irish peasants were living on tiny squares of land, subsisting almost solely on a diet of potatoes. Conservative estimates place the Irish population at eight million at that time, though the Irish hated census takers, so there were probably far more.

The Anglo-Irish Protestant ascendancy ruled the country from their mansions dotting the countryside, collecting rents from the tenants—sometimes in the form of vegetables other than potatoes, which they exported—and enjoying a high life.

In 1842, a fungus that attacked potatoes arrived in Ireland from America. Although the potatoes were whole and seemingly fine when dug, within days they turned to a foul, rotting mush that was completely inedible and stank abominably. Nearly eight million people on an island smaller than the state of Indiana found themselves with nothing to eat.

Evictions became commonplace as many landlords saw this disaster as a heaven-sent opportunity to rid their land of its "pestilence." All across Ireland, starving Irishmen, unable to pay their rents, were thrown out of their homes and their humble cottages were burned before their eyes.

And if Nature weren't cruel enough, the winter of 1846–47 was one of the most bitter on record. Hundreds of thousands of destitute peasants huddled together for warmth in ditches, caves, and holes dug in the frozen ground. Sanitation was difficult, and fevers raged, taking countless lives.

Even at the height of the famine, the landlords continued their business as usual, exporting pork, beef, lamb, barley, oats, wheat, and vegetables that could have fed the starving masses. Wagons laden with food rumbled down roads on their way to the seaports, passing ditches filled with the skeletal corpses of people.

When Sir Robert Peel, the British home secretary, was told the magnitude of the disaster, he dismissed the information as "the Irishman's eternal tendency to exaggerate Irish news." He did send some Indian corn, which did more harm than good. The peasants had no mills to grind it, and the stuff was impossible to cook or digest.

Some Anglo-Protestants saw the situation as a chance to convert the "heathen Catholics." The price of a meal at their soup kitchens was the rejection of the Catholic faith and the embracing of Protestantism. Those who traded their religion for soup were known as "soupers" and were hated by those who chose death rather than surrender their faith.

Conservative estimates say that one million of the Irish found their way aboard "coffin ships," bound for other parts of the world, primarily the United States. In the holds of these ships, so many of the half-starved, diseased people died in transit that it has been said, "The floor of the Atlantic is littered with Irish bones."

When it was all over, Ireland had lost at least three and a half million of her children to death and emigration. A lesser people might have lost their souls as well, their spirit, their love of life. Our forebears endured, for which we can all be proud.

# 41

# Maria Edgeworth

## (1767–1849)

Certainly Anglo landlords of Ireland have attained an unsavory reputation over the years, and, in most cases, not without due cause. This was especially so in the famine years of the 1840s (see CHAPTER 40). But many of the Anglo-Irish property owners, the landed gentry of that time, were compassionate, generous, and highly sympathetic to the plight of the peasantry. One such person was a writer named Maria Edgeworth.

Maria was born on January 1, 1767, the third eldest of twenty-two children sired by Richard Lovell Edgeworth with the first of his four wives.

As a child and a young woman, Maria developed a deep understanding of and affection for the Irish peasantry. She saw the pain and suffering inflicted on tenants by landlords who were less progressive and compassionate in their policies than she and her father were.

Having collaborated with her father on *Essays on Practical Education* and *Essays on Irish Bulls,* Maria discovered she had a talent for writing. Her first novel, *Castle Rackrent,* published in 1800, portrayed the pain and havoc created by irresponsible landlords—in this case, the Rackrent family.

The book was an enormous success in Ireland and in England. For the first time, novels about Ireland became fashionable, as the British public learned about its island neighbor.

In her subsequent novels, *Ennui* (1809) and *The Absentee* (1812), Maria continued to denounce negligent landlords. But her style was so humorous, the morals of her stories presented with such a light, non-judgmental touch, that they were readily accepted by her readership.

Maria was seventy-eight when the Great Hunger struck Ireland in 1845. Even at that age, she was a fervent advocate of the Irish peasants. She used the remainder of the Edgeworth family's finances, as well as her own time and energies, to plead their cause to the world. In return for her efforts, she received enormous amounts of money and goods for distribution to the destitute.

The tireless campaign took its toll on the elderly woman, as did the pain of seeing all the misery that she was still unable to prevent. The tiny lady with the big heart died on May 22, 1849, at the age of eighty-two.

# 42

# Irish Wit

The Irish are certainly known for their wit. And that isn't always as complimentary as we might hope. Sure, we can be a funny and entertaining lot. It's one of our greatest virtues—surpassed only by our humility. But our wit is a double-edged sword that can slice and dice a foe quicker than he can dodge the blow.

In the olden days, when bards made a living of spinning poems for their kings, they spent only half their time praising their nobles. The rest was spent insulting the king's enemies. So the put-down has become a highly refined tradition among the bards of Ireland. And on a Saturday night in the local pub, every Irishman is a bard.

But not all their humor is dark. Some is merely insightful. Sometimes the speaker is laughing at himself more than at anyone else. On occasion the epigram is merely an observation about life. Here are some distinctly Irish witticisms for your pleasure:

An inch is a great deal in a man's nose.

He would skin a louse and send the hide and fat to market.

It's the first drop that destroyed me, there's no harm at all in the last.

He would go to mass every day if holy water were whiskey.

Only the Lord can make a racehorse out of a jackass.

The losing horse blames the saddle.

Put an Irishman on a spit and you'll find two more to turn him.

An Irishman is never at peace except when he's fighting.

Long sleep makes a bare backside.

Never make a toil of pleasure, the man said as he dug his wife's grave three feet deep.

# 43

# Charles Stewart Parnell

## (1846–1891)

This Protestant from the landlord class came close to winning the prize of Home Rule for Ireland, and probably would have succeeded, but for ill health and his love of a married woman.

Although he was born into a well-to-do family in 1846 and received his education in England, Parnell was taught at an early age the evils of British imperialism. His father had fought England in 1812 as an admiral. His mother was American. Staunchly anti-British, she made her views abundantly clear to her son, who not surprisingly adopted her beliefs.

In 1867, at the age of only twenty-one, Parnell found himself in sympathy with the Fenians, a society who believed in forcing Britain to grant Ireland her independence through military force. While he agreed with them in principle, he felt the Home Rule party offered the same ideology with less extreme measures.

Parnell led an agitation (Irish term for a vigorous movement) for Home Rule, which would include an assembly in Ireland with some limited powers of government in Irish affairs. Using his narrowly circumscribed "authority," he fought within the House of Commons until two bills regarding Home Rule were introduced. Both bills were defeated, but thanks to Parnell's spirited campaign, Home Rule had become a major issue in British politics.

Unfortunately, Parnell never saw the fruition of his dream. He became romantically involved with a married woman, Mrs. Kitty O'Shea, wife of Captain William O'Shea, an Irish Home Rule member of Parliament. When the husband named Parnell as the adulterous third party in his divorce action against his wife, the resulting scandal caused such an uproar that Parnell's reputation, credibility, and career were destroyed.

In 1891, as Parnell traveled frantically across Ireland, trying to rally the support that had been withdrawn from him because of the scandal, his health began to suffer. Although his doctor forbade it, he delivered a speech bareheaded in the pouring rain in County Galway. His arm was in a sling, badly crippled by rheumatism. Parnell died a week after the speech. He was simply worn out, his life energy spent at the age of forty-five.

# 44

# Irish Wisdom

Hearing a bit of Irish wisdom will sometimes cause you to chuckle and will often make you think.

Whether it be a wee warning from a "wise person" from Kerry, or an observation from a fiddle-playing tinker from Cork, it's worth your consideration. Here are a few:

You can't whistle and chew at the same time.

Don't give cherries to pigs; don't give advice to fools.

Don't see all you see and don't hear all you hear.

Never scald your lips with another man's porridge.

Don't show all your teeth until you can bite.

Don't be breakin' your shin on a stool that's not in your way.

Neither speak well nor ill of yourself.

Don't yield to the Saxon, but beat him well.

It's a bad thing not to have a story on the tip of your tongue.

When fools make mistakes, they lay the blame on Providence.

There are two things that can't be cured—death and the want of sense.

# 45

# The Emigrants
## (1845–1891)

Between the years 1845 and 1891, three million Irish came to America. Fleeing the horrors of the Great Hunger (see CHAPTER 40) and other forms of persecution, they crowded aboard the wretched "coffin ships" and took their chances in a new land.

Unfortunately, their new country didn't always treat them better than the old one. After the rigors of the disease-ridden ships, many were sick, most were poor, and hardly any had marketable skills. In Ireland their existence had been fairly simple. The raising of potatoes was a rudimentary exercise, requiring little expertise. Few had trades with which to make a living for their families.

No sooner were they off the ships than they were beset by opportunists, ready to rob them of what meager possessions they still had or to exploit them in many other creative, despicable ways. Swindlers of all breeds discovered that they could hang around the docks wearing a bit of green and speaking with a hackneyed Irish brogue, and those disembarking would be their sheep for the fleecing.

As enthusiastically as the cheats sought the Irish, the remainder of the population avoided them. Signs that read NO IRISH NEED APPLY hung in shops and storefronts in New York, Boston, and other ports of entry.

But we can be proud of our forefathers and mothers for their courage in standing against the odds. Yes, some of them behaved in ways that fostered the stereotype of the drunken, brawling Irish who filled the slums to overflowing. Old police records reveal that the Irish may have been involved in more than their share of drink-related fistfights. However, their contribution to the crime rate for serious offenses like murder was well below average.

Many of the Irish chose not to remain in the inner cities but to adventure beyond to the American frontier. A large number traveled to the Oklahoma Territory, where they settled and farmed the land. They also participated in the California gold rush, the building of the railroads, and the construction of many major bridges and trestles linking the East with the West.

Many Irish immigrants became involved with American politics. Smooth talk wasn't the only gift they possessed that made them good politicians. For centuries the Irish had been arbitrating disagreements between opposing factions, striking balances and making peace where there had been war (see CHAPTER 5). These skills were essential for politicians in cities with culturally diverse populations.

They were also gifted athletes, specifically in the then-popular sport of boxing. John L. Sullivan (see CHAPTER 62), Gene Tunney, and Jack Doyle were among the best-known boxers of their day. National pride ran high, and the Irish took great satisfaction in seeing their fighters pummel an Italian or Jewish fellow and win a victory for old Eire.

The Irish supplied much precious manpower in the form of soldiers for American wars (see CHAPTER 59). The passion they had shown in defending Ireland was easily transferred to the United States of America. They were as willing to shed blood in the defense of their new land as ever before.

For a country so small, Ireland contributed much to the societies where her children settled, bringing her warmth, wit, and inimitable charm to many a foreign shore.

# 46

# William Butler Yeats

## (1865–1939)

The first Irishman to win the Nobel Prize for Literature, W. B. Yeats was known as the father of the Irish literary revival that occurred between 1891 and 1921. His plays, poetry, and prose defined the Irish people and their Celtic heritage.

Novelist Katherine Tynan described Yeats as "a gaunt young figure, mouthing poetry, swinging his arms and gesticulating as he went." He confused the local police, who weren't sure if he presented a threat to public safety with his eccentricities. But they generally left him alone, saying, "Sure 'tisn't mad he is, nor with drink. 'Tis the poetry that's disturbin' his head."

Yeats was born in Dublin on June 13, 1865, the oldest son of an Anglo-Irish artist, John Butler Yeats. Oscar Wilde's father, Sir William

Wilde, described Yeats's family as "the cleverest and most spirited people I have ever met."

First published in the *Dublin University Review* in 1885, Yeats went on to pen an enormous and brilliant body of work, consisting of poetry, prose, plays, and political commentaries. Fascinated by Celtic mythology, Yeats published *The Celtic Twilight* in 1893, a collection of Irish tales and folklore, and many of his writings centered around the mystic world, inhabited by fairy and ghost spirits.

In 1915, he was offered a knighthood, but like a number of patriotic Irishmen before him, he refused the British honor on principle. When he won the Nobel Prize in 1923, they say he celebrated by eating sausages.

From 1922 to 1928, Yeats was a member of the Senate in the newly established Irish Free State. But his liberal political views were highly controversial. He even proposed legislation that would allow divorce, making him unpopular with the Church and his more conservative contemporaries.

Yeats was a founding member of the Irish National Literary Society and, with his friend Lady Gregory, formed the Irish Literary Theatre Society. In 1904, it moved into the Abbey Theatre in Dublin and presented plays that both intrigued and inflamed audiences unaccustomed to Yeats's less than traditional views.

In one of his plays, *Cathleen ni Houlihan,* Yeats cast in the leading role a beautiful, spirited woman named Maud Gonne. Maud was quite the activist, supporting the causes of the poor in the slums of Dublin. Yeats fell in love with Maud, but his affection was unrequited.

In 1903, he conducted a tour across the United States, speaking to forty enthralled audiences, and when he returned, Maud had married another. Her husband was killed in the Easter Rising of 1916, and Yeats proposed marriage to her. When she refused, Yeats turned his attention and affections to her daughter, the beautiful, young Iseult Gonne, and she, too, rejected his proposal. But one lady did accept his offer of matrimony—the intelligent, vivacious Georgie Hyde-Lees. The match fulfilled Yeats's obsession with the spirit world, as Georgie was said to be a medium. Together they explored the occult, even attending seances.

Some of Yeats's best-known pieces include *Poems and Ballads of Young Ireland,* coedited with Douglas Hyde, *The Wanderings of Oisin, Crossways,* and the play *Cathleen ni Houlihan.* One of his last and most ambitious tasks was the editing of *The Oxford Book of Poetry* in 1936.

On January 4, 1939, Yeats wrote: "I know for certain that my time will not be long, yet I am happy, and I think full of an energy, of an energy I had despaired of. It seems to me that I have found what I wanted." He died twenty-four days later at the age of seventy-four, and was buried in the shadow of the magnificent mountain Benbulben, in Drumcliff, near Sligo. His gravestone bears the epitaph he wrote: "Cast a cold eye on life, on death. Horseman, pass by."

# 47

# Ghosts of Ireland

If you have ever walked through a forest in Ireland, with bluebells at your feet, the smell of the earthy loam filling your head, and the sound of a trickling creek in the distance, you can almost swear that you aren't alone. Somewhere, maybe from behind that stone carpeted with velvety green moss, someone is watching.

Those who believe in ghosts have numerous explanations for the phenomenon. Many think they are disembodied spirits who have somehow lost their way, unable to continue on to their eternal destination. The reason for their wanderings may be a desire for revenge against someone who was responsible for their death, or they may have an affection for some person or place here in this life that they are unable to release.

Other, more scientific "ghostbusters" theorize that these apparitions are not actual entities but some sort of residual energy, left behind after a human being experienced a high level of emotional trauma, such as being murdered or dying violently in some other way.

If murder or unexpected death could cause a haunting, then it is little wonder that Ireland would be densely inhabited by a ghostly population. The grim observation has been made that the grass is so green because it has been well fertilized with innocent blood over thousands of years. Almost every shadowed glen, every sunlit rolling hill, every sandy beach and cloud-capped mountaintop has been the scene of some terrible injustice.

Rather than live in fear of their ethereal neighbors, the Irish take it all in stride and approach the matter the way they do everything else, with practicality. Believing that many ghosts need help from the living, the Irish are quick to offer a compassionate blessing to a troubled soul to send it on its way.

One tradition born of kindness and respect, two qualities foremost in the Irish character, is that of carrying a bit of bread in your pocket when you intend to cross a field of "Hungry Grass." This is a meadow known to be a place where people perished, trying to eat the grass, during the Great Hunger (see CHAPTER 40), the terrible potato famine of 1845–49. The piece of bread is carried to commemorate their tragedy and honor their memory.

In the end, it can be said that the Irish are a compassionate people, to the living *and* to the dead.

# 48

# The Abbey Theatre
(1904–1951)

The Irish see the stage and the dramas presented there as expressions of their nation's mind and heart. The theater is far more than mere entertainment to the Irish; it has been a voice that has informed and enlightened the world about the Irish people and their causes.

And the birthplace of fine Irish theater was the Abbey Theatre in Dublin.

In 1904 the National Dramatic Company and the Irish Literary Theatre Society merged to form what would become the Abbey Theatre. The Abbey opened on December 27, 1904, with *On Baile's Strand* by William Butler Yeats and *Spreading the News* by Lady Gregory.

Many of the Abbey's plays had nationalist themes, but none more than Yeats's *Cathleen ni Houlihan*. In the story, Ireland was symbolized by the character of an old woman who convinced a young man to leave his home and loved ones to sacrifice his life for Ireland. Yeats's stirring words, spoken by the extraordinary actress Maud Gonne, stirred audiences to such a high level of emotion that the play was credited with inspiring the rebel patriots to revolt in the Easter Rising of 1916 (see Chapter 69).

In keeping with the tradition of the ancient Irish bards, poetry and politics have always been tightly interwoven in Ireland, so it was no surprise that the stage was used as a forum for nationalist ideals. In fact, this became so much the norm that when creative new dramatists like John Millington Synge presented plays that went against the nationalists' ideal, they caused riots in the streets.

In Synge's *Playboy of the Western World,* produced by the Abbey in 1907, the Irish peasantry was portrayed as sympathetic but flawed, which inflamed the public, who thought they were being ridiculed. But W. B. Yeats and theater codirector Lady Gregory defended Synge's genius and right of artistic expression, as well as those other dramatists, like the brilliant but controversial Sean O' Casey, who would follow twenty years later.

Unfortunately, the Abbey Theatre was lost to fire in 1951. But the tradition continued, and the National Dramatic Company was moved to the Queen's Theatre; then in 1966 it was moved again, to its present location in Lower Abbey Street.

# 49

# The Building of America

It is no coincidence that between 1840 and 1860, the peak years of famine and postfamine emigration from Ireland, massive building and expansion occurred in the United States. Skyscrapers were erected in New York. The Brooklyn Bridge was built, a wonder of technology in the nineteenth century, which linked the ever-expanding New York City to Brooklyn and Long Island. The flood of famine victims arriving in the United States provided the manpower needed to raise the incredible structures that still stand today.

In 1840, before the Irish began to arrive in such large numbers, there were only three thousand miles of railroad tracks in the United States. By 1860, the East and West coasts were connected by thirty thousand miles of rails. And while it was backbreaking and dangerous, railroad work provided a way for Irish immigrants to escape the slums of the eastern seaboard cities and travel to the newly settled West.

When the city center of Chicago was destroyed by the fire of 1871, it was mostly Irish hands that rebuilt it. And, as with all of the other construction projects of that time, safety measures for workers were widely ignored and countless lives were lost. Many a man born on Irish soil ended his life in a grave of cement while building this country's dams, bridges, canals, and roads.

The factories of the Northeast ushered America into the Industrial Age, and those plants and mills were filled with Irish men and women. They labored hard and long, most without complaint, because—as difficult as their lot might be—their new lives were better than the horrors they had left behind in their beloved but ravaged Ireland.

And the Irish continue to build this nation—though now, CEOs of great corporations conduct their business in penthouse offices in the very skyscrapers built by their forefathers.

# 50

# Augusta, Lady Gregory

## (1852–1932)

Folklorist and playwright Lady Gregory had three burning ambitions in her life: to revive the flagging Irish language and Irish literature, to establish an Irish literary theater, and to use the language, literature, and theater to prepare the Irish people for assuming the responsibilities of independence.

Isabella Augusta Persse was born at Roxborough, County Galway, on March 15, 1852, to a gentleman farmer and his wife. From her Irish-speaking maid, the young Isabella heard stories of Ireland's mythical folk heroes and heroines, as well as poems that extolled the dream of Irish independence from the British.

On March 4, 1880, the twenty-seven-year-old Isabella Augusta married her neighbor Sir William Gregory, a man thirty-five years her senior. Sir William had served as the British colonial governor of Ceylon. The couple traveled frequently, and they had one son, William Robert.

After her husband's death in 1892, Lady Gregory focused her energies on her writing. She visited the humble cottages of the Irish countryside, listening to the peasants' stories and recording them for posterity. She published a number of these collections: *A Book of Saints and Wonders* (1906), *The Kiltartan History Book* (1909), and *Visions and Beliefs in the West of Ireland* (1920).

When she met William Butler Yeats in 1896 at the home of a mutual friend, she found a spirit as enthralled with these mystical tales as her own. They collaborated on projects such as *Fairy and Folk Tales of the Irish Peasantry.* But the crowning glory of their joint efforts was the founding of the great Abbey Theatre. Lady Gregory had a keen eye for talent and is credited with discovering the great Sean O'Casey. When O'Casey's work generated controversy with its irreverent views of Irish character, she defended him. Whether she liked a playwright, or his work, Lady Gregory championed the rights of artists against censorship.

At the age of fifty she wrote the first of her forty-plus plays, *Kincora,* of which Yeats said, "This play gives me the greatest joy—colour, speech, all has music." George Bernard Shaw called her *Shanwalla* one of the best ghost plays he had ever seen.

She and Yeats remained close friends until her death at her home, Coole Park, on May 22, 1932. Her last writing was a note scribbled on her deathbed, thanking him.

# 51

# Sean O'Casey

## (1880–1964)

The Dublin slums of the 1880s were a dreadful place for a poor child to be raised. But Sean O'Casey survived a hideous childhood and achieved celebrity and critical acclaim by bringing those dark days alive in his plays. He was considered a crude genius whose main strength as a writer lay in his ability to switch deftly from comedy to tragedy.

Sean O'Casey was born John Casey in Dublin on March 30, 1880, the youngest of thirteen children in a poor Protestant family. When the father, Michael Casey, died, the family went from bad to worse; only five of the children survived to adulthood. O'Casey himself was plagued with severe vision problems all his life, probably due to a desperate lack of nutrition and medical care. His school attendance suffered because of his affliction, and he was a teenager before he could read.

But once he discovered the world of books, there was no stopping him. His other great passion was the political arena, specifically that of the labor movement. He joined the political arm of the Irish Transport and General Workers' Union, known as the Irish Citizen Army, and wrote for its paper, the *Irish Worker.*

Upon taking part in an amateur production at the Empire Theatre, his interest in the theater grew, and he tried his hand at writing a few short plays. In 1923, when he was forty-three, the great Abbey Theatre produced his play *The Shadow of a Gunman,* and for the first time the grim reality of life in Dublin's slums was presented onstage. O'Casey's ironic wit, his lively dialogue, his warm but incisive style, and the unique subject matter made the play an instant success.

In 1924, O'Casey enjoyed his second major success as the Abbey produced his three-act play about the Irish Civil War, *Juno and the Paycock.* Again, O'Casey's style—combining hysterical comedy with shocking tragedy—proved highly successful with audiences.

But O'Casey wasn't prepared for the sharp condemnation he would receive upon the debut of his third effort, *The Plough and the Stars.* An ambitious project, the play covered the subject of the Easter Rising of 1916, from the beginnings of the ill-fated bid for Irish freedom from the British to the tragic ending of the short-lived revolution.

Believing that his work ridiculed Irish patriotism, even the Irish themselves, crowds rioted just as they had at the opening of John Synge's *Playboy of the Western World,* twenty years before. So unruly was the audience in expressing its disapproval that William Butler Yeats himself was moved to take the stage and declare in O'Casey's defense, "You have disgraced yourselves again. Is this to be an ever-recurring celebration of the arrival of Irish genius?"

Hurt and angry, O'Casey left Ireland and traveled to London, where he remained for the rest of his life, returning to Ireland only for brief visits. In 1927, when he was forty-seven, he married a young Irish actress, Eileen Reynolds, and they had three children.

By the age of eighty-four, O'Casey was almost completely blind. He suffered a second heart attack and died on September 18, 1964, at Devon. O'Casey will always be considered one of Ireland's great dramatists, a rough-and-tumble intellectual, the working man's bard.

# 52

# George Bernard Shaw

## (1856–1950)

Considering his less than humble beginnings, few would have guessed that the lad born on Upper Synge Street in Dublin on July 26, 1856, would become a great orator whose speeches on socialism would influence the masses. He would become a renowned critic of art, music, and drama, and his plays would still be enjoyed by theater lovers a year after his death.

When he was forty-two years old, Shaw wrote of himself, "I have been dinning into the public head that I am an extraordinarily witty, brilliant and clever man. That is now part of the public opinion of England; and no power in heaven or on Earth will ever change it." And while he, no doubt, wrote this with tongue in cheek, he couldn't have stated the facts more truthfully.

Shaw was born into a Protestant Dublin family, the third child of

George Carr Shaw, a wholesale grain merchant and an alcoholic who neglected both his business and his family. His mother, Elizabeth Gurly Shaw, may have been considered cold and humorless, but she had an avid love of music, which she imparted to her children. And, although the young George was a poor student in school—said to be near or at the bottom of his class—he was well versed in classical music at an early age. He left school at the age of fifteen and became a clerk in a land agency in Dublin.

At seventeen, Shaw followed his mother and sister to London, where he spent most of his time in the reading room of the British Museum, writing novels. He had little talent for it and wrote in an outdated, early Victorian style. None was successful.

In 1884, Shaw joined the Fabian Society, a new group dedicated to the advancement of socialism through intellectual rather than violent means. While campaigning with the Fabians, the shy, reserved Shaw developed his magnificent oratory skills. Tall and thin with a red beard, he presented a convincing image of a man of letters when he stood before an enthralled audience.

A year later, he became a book reviewer for the *Pall Mall Gazette*, and this job led to others for various periodicals, where he critiqued not only books but also art and music.

The first of Shaw's many plays, *Widowers' Houses*, was performed in 1892. In its story, one of the characters has to deal with the knowledge that her mother made her fortune through prostitution. As a dramatist, Shaw's intention was to use his writing as a means of social commentary. He wrote what he called "unpleasant plays," unpleasant because they forced the audience to look at subjects that were distasteful, offensive, or controversial. Shaw wanted the public to reconsider its staid, conventional views and to open its collective mind to new possibilities, especially in the arena of social reform.

In 1898, Shaw married Charlotte Payne-Townshend, an Irish heiress who had faithfully attended him during a serious illness that year. Much later she would prompt him to write a play about Joan of Arc. He did so, and in 1926, at the age of seventy, Shaw received the Nobel Prize for *Saint Joan*.

Among his fifty-plus plays, some of his best-known dramas were "pleasant" plays about the follies of romance: *Candida, The Man of Destiny, Arms and the Man,* and *You Can Never Tell.* Perhaps his most famous work, *Pygmalion,* was the predecessor of the popular Broadway movie and musical *My Fair Lady.* However, the romantic ending of the movie was not what Shaw intended, as he saw no love affair existing between Eliza Doolittle and her difficult professor, Henry Higgins.

Although Shaw lived to the age of ninety-four, the proclaimed vegetarian and teetotaler remained active, mentally and physically. He died in 1950 from complications resulting from a fall from an apple tree he had been pruning.

# 53

# A "Comely" People

While it might be considered less than humble for a person of Irish descent to say so, the sons and daughters of auld Eire are, indeed, a comely people. (More handsome, it seems, than humble.)

Over the ages, the waves of invaders who swept across Ireland contributed their hearty, robust genes to the pool, creating a lively population. The long-limbed, athletic Celts, the sturdy, fiery Spaniards, and the gold- and copper-haired, blue- and green-eyed Vikings all left their mark on the Irish people. And what a charming mixture they created!

Before the Great Famine, when the health of the Irish was severely compromised, they were known throughout Europe as an extremely attractive folk. Primarily living on potatoes and milk, a diet that contains all the nutrients necessary to nurture the human body, they thrived. The British who visited Ireland expected to find a peaked, haggard peasantry but returned home with stories of ruddy complexions, sparkling eyes, vigorous constitutions, and enthusiastic spirits.

Contemporary visitors find the same when they alight from ship or plane on the Enchanted Isle. Where else can you see eyes the colors of emeralds, tourmalines, and peridots, not to mention all the marvelous shades of blue from sapphire to aquamarine? Even the Scandinavian countries cannot claim as many shades of gold and copper hair.

Walking the streets of Limerick and other historically Norse settlements, you will see lasses with auburn hair that has a rich, almost blue sheen . . . reminiscent, no doubt, of their Viking ancestors. While traveling about the countryside, you may also notice the strange but delightful combination of dark hair and light skin, a result of those Spaniards who washed ashore after the sinking of their Armada.

Even Irish immigrants have gained the reputation for being big, bold lads and lasses. The stereotype of the Irish cop—a burly, no-nonsense sort of chap—is well earned. Tall, muscular, and athletic, the Irish have always made good soldiers.

So if you're of Irish descent and are considered a handsome lad or a well-balanced lass (a term denoting a female with a shapely figure), you can thank your lucky Irish genes. Oh, yes—and if you're a wee bit less than humble about your good looks, that seems to come with the territory too.

# 54

# Hurling

Although Gaelic football is extremely popular in Ireland, no sport is more distinctly Irish than the ancient game of hurling. It is the fastest of team sports, a rough-and-tumble game for "manly men," which suits the Irish temperament perfectly. But in spite of the game's violence, serious injuries seldom occur.

According to legend, the mythical warrior Cuchulain and other champions of old were excellent hurlers. Whoever originated the game, it has been played in Ireland since before recorded history. In 1884, the Gaelic Athletic Association was formed, and it established the rules of the game.

Two fifteen-member teams play on a field that is 90 yards wide and 150 yards long. A ball, called a slitter, is caught on a stick, a hurley, and hurled to the goal. The slitter has a cork center covered with leather and is between nine and ten inches in circumference. The hurley is a narrow stick about three and a half feet long with a curved blade that is approximately three inches wide.

At each end of the field is a goal, formed by two posts about twenty-one feet high, set twenty-one feet apart and connected by a crossbar set eight feet above the ground. A net is stretched across the goal, attached to the crossbar and the lower posts. The players catch the slitter on the blade of the hurley and hurl it into the goal. Three points are scored when the slitter goes into the net, and one point if it is hurled between the posts but over the crossbar.

Hurling is played almost exclusively in the Republic of Ireland, and the All-Ireland championship competition is held every year, as it has been since 1887. That event is the Irish equivalent to the U.S. Super Bowl. Champion hurlers are national heroes, and Irish lads dream of growing up and leading their team to victory.

# 55

# Oscar Wilde

(1854–1900)

Oscar Wilde epitomized Irish wit and became famous, then infamous, when his flamboyant, unconventional lifestyle landed him in prison. He was convicted of sodomy, which was a crime in Victorian England. Serving his sentence cost Wilde his health and, ultimately, his life. He died in poverty and dishonor, leaving a comet's blaze of brilliant words as his legacy.

Wilde was born in Dublin in 1854 to well-to-do parents. His father was a writer and a brilliant surgeon; his mother, Lady Jane Wilde, was also celebrated for her writing. Like his literary parents, Wilde showed early promise as a writer, winning prizes for his poetry at Trinity College, Dublin, and Magdalen College, Oxford.

A passionate romantic, Wilde pursued a number of beautiful women, including actresses Lily Langtry and Ellen Terry, and the lovely

Florence Balcombe, who later married Bram Stoker. But he ultimately married the daughter of a respectable family in Ireland, Constance Lloyd.

Although Wilde was quite extravagant in his praise of his wife, his marriage did not continue to be a happy one. In 1891, when Wilde was thirty-seven and at the peak of his creative genius, having published the highly successful novel *The Picture of Dorian Gray,* he met Lord Alfred Douglas. Douglas was a handsome but arrogant, self-centered fellow. He encouraged enmity between Wilde and Douglas's father, the marquis of Queensberry. The marquis loathed Wilde and strongly condemned his son's relationship with the famous writer, who openly associated with male prostitutes.

In spite of his personal conflicts, Wilde's career flourished. The next year, his play *Lady Windermere's Fan* was produced in London, establishing him as a popular playwright as well as a novelist. This was followed by other plays, distinctive for their marvelously witty dialogue: *A Woman of No Importance, An Ideal Husband,* and, perhaps his greatest work of all, *The Importance of Being Earnest.*

Meanwhile, thanks to Douglas, the hostilities between Wilde and the marquis escalated. On February 18, 1895, the marquis left a card at his club, which was blatantly addressed, "Oscar Wilde posing as a sodomite." Furious, Wilde sued him for libel. This was a great risk for Wilde. But risk it he did. And shortly after the jury found the marquis not guilty of libel, Wilde was arrested and convicted of the charge of sodomy. He was sentenced to two years at hard labor . . . an arduous ordeal for a gentleman unaccustomed to physically strenuous work.

Wilde retained his sense of humor, even under difficult circumstances. As he was led to prison, handcuffed, without coat or hat for protection from the driving rain, he said, "If this is the way Queen Victoria treats her convicts, she doesn't deserve to have any."

His time in prison took a serious toll on Wilde's health and financial status. After his release, he would live only three more years, residing in Paris.

In the fall of 1900, Wilde became desperately ill with cerebral meningitis. He rallied himself in his sickroom enough to complain that he hated the wallpaper. "It's killing me," he said. "One of us has to go!" Just before expiring, he woke briefly from a coma to hear a couple of physicians discussing his mounting medical expenses. He said, "I am dying as I have lived . . . beyond my means."

In perhaps the final irony, on November 30, 1900, the man who had lived his life as an agnostic asked on his deathbed to be received into the Roman Catholic Church. He was.

# 56

# Irish Insults

A well-worded, sharp-edged insult is a work of art and has been highly regarded in Irish culture since the times of the ancient Celts. One of the reasons the bards of olden days held so much power in Celtic society was that they could destroy your reputation with one brilliantly composed song or poem, expounding your cowardice, dishonesty, or ignorance (see CHAPTER 6). Even today, the Irish enjoy nothing so much as a quick-witted verbal jab to the solar plexus of the enemy's ego. Following are a few classics:

At a party a boring fellow once told Oscar Wilde, "I passed your house yesterday." To which Wilde replied, "Thank you so much."

Oscar Wilde once said of George Bernard Shaw, "Shaw hasn't an enemy in the world. But none of his friends like him."

As George Bernard Shaw sat listening to a string quartet he found less than inspiring, a friend told him, "You know, they've been playing together for twelve years." Shaw returned, "Surely we have been here longer than that."

When poet Patrick Kavanagh neglected to buy a lady a drink at a bar, she snapped, "Did you not see I had a mouth on me?" He replied, "Sure, how could I miss it, and it swinging between your two ears like a skippin' rope?"

James Joyce was extolled for his writing, but never for his humility. On one occasion, Joyce told a group that he intended to "forge in the smithy of my soul the uncreated conscience of my race." A less-than-impressed listener asked, "And when did you decide to have it mass-produced in plastic?"

George Bernard Shaw made no bones about his dislike for critics. Once he telephoned a lad who had panned one of his plays and told the critic, "I am sitting in the smallest room in the house. I have your review before me. It will soon be behind me."

# 57

# James McNeill Whistler

(1834–1903)

James Whistler was a progressive, highly original artist, one of the first European artists to incorporate Oriental elements into his work. So popular were his paintings, etchings, and lithographs that Oriental art became the rage in Victorian England and beyond, the mark of sophistication and taste. But it is one of his portraits he is best known for, a simple painting of his mother. The portrait, called *Whistler's Mother,* painted in 1872, hangs in the Louvre in Paris.

Whistler was born on July 10, 1834, in Lowell, Massachusetts. When he was nine years old, his father, a military engineer, moved the family to St. Petersburg, Russia, then to Moscow, where he was building a railroad.

From 1851 to 1854, Whistler attended West Point; then he proceeded to Paris to study art. When he moved to London in 1859, he gained a reputation as much for being a dandy as for his art. He moved in eccentric social circles, including those of the flamboyant writer Oscar Wilde. The witty Whistler once said something particularly clever to Wilde, and Wilde remarked, "Oh, James, I wish I had said that." To which Whistler dryly replied, "You will, Oscar. You will."

Although he was terribly popular with the public at large, Whistler didn't always receive accolades from art critics. He sued one for referring to his *Nocturne* series as "flinging a pot of paint in the public's face." Whistler won but received only one farthing in damages.

In the later years of his life, Whistler devoted more time to his notorious reputation than to his work and became a cult figure, known for his eccentric clothing, his affected speech and gestures, and his face makeup. But his art was undoubtedly some of the most beloved of his time.

# 58

# Maud Gonne

(1866–1953)

Many Irishmen considered Maud Gonne, an actress who received much fame and acclaim from her roles on stage at the Abbey Theatre, the most beautiful woman in Ireland in her day. But Maud Gonne was so much more than a pretty face. She was a spitfire who used her beauty and her passionate nature to further the cause of freedom for the Irish.

Considering her privileged upbringing—her father was an Irish officer in the British army—one might have assumed Maud would be spoiled. But at an early age, she expressed her own opinions, which were in direct variance to her parents', and pledged her life to the cause of Irish freedom.

Already a stunning beauty at the age of seventeen, she was presented to Albert Edward, prince of Wales, at the Viceregal Court in Dublin Castle. During a ball there, the prince was so taken by her beauty that he escorted her to the platform. The feisty young lady took full advantage of the situation. She entertained the royal court by singing "The Wearin' o' the Green."

Maud chose to fight not only for political reform but also against poverty and sickness in the slums of Dublin. In 1900, she founded the Daughters of Erin, a group of equally "radical" women bent upon accomplishing the same goals.

William Butler Yeats was another man who was completely smitten with the lovely Maud. He fell madly in love with her, making her the star of his renowned play *Cathleen ni Houlihan.* He was bitterly disappointed to hear she had married Major John MacBride in 1903 in Paris, at the age of thirty-seven. When MacBride was executed for his part in the Easter Rising thirteen years later, Yeats proposed matrimony to her, but she refused, telling him that marriage to him would be "such a dull affair."

Her husband's death made her all the more emphatic about her mission. For the remainder of her days she worked on behalf of the republicans, fighting for an independent Ireland. She was imprisoned during the Irish Civil War in January 1923, where she went on a hunger strike and was released after twenty days.

Maud is remembered not for her beauty, or even for her ability as an actress, but for the way she spent her time, her energy, and her talents in the pursuit of a free Ireland.

# 59

# Ireland's Sons, America's Soldiers

If you can believe the complaints of the British in the 1700s, it was a batch of transplanted Irishmen who stirred up the trouble among the colonists that led to that irritating declaration in 1776.

And they may have been right.

There were plenty of Irish on American soil at the time. According to the first census of 1790, those who had been born in Ireland or were of direct Irish ancestry totaled 194,000, out of a population of 4,000,000. And heaven knows, they harbored no great affection for the British. So it's only natural that they would encourage the disgruntled colonists to rid themselves, if possible, of Mother England.

Among those who signed the Declaration of Independence, four had been born in Ireland and five had Irish heritage. At least twenty-two members of the first Continental Congress were Irish.

And when the actual fighting of the Revolutionary War got underway, the Irish were front and center, in the thick of it.

Some of the outstanding soldiers who fought for American independence were General Edward Hand, General John Sullivan of Limerick, Captain John Barry, commander of the *Lexington,* and Colonel Stephen Moylan of County Cork. So many Irishmen fought for the Americans that two witnesses testified before the British House of Commons that half the Continental Army was from Ireland. While the House of Commons was digesting this unsavory tidbit, Lord Mountjoy complained bitterly, "We have lost America to the Irish!"

During the War Between the States, the Irish soldiers were known for their compassion on the battlefield. They often nursed the wounded among the enemy and were merciful to prisoners of war, even sharing rations when food and supplies were scarce. One distinguished Confederate soldier said he preferred to go to battle with an Irish soldier because of his courage, his endurance, cleanliness, and cheerfulness, and because he was more amenable to discipline—the latter being a bit outside the stereotype of the feisty, rebellious Irishman.

# 60

# John Millington Synge
## (1871–1909)

John Millington Synge is considered by many to be the greatest playwright to emerge from the Irish literary renaissance that occurred between 1891 and 1921. But Synge was a humble man who claimed to have received his best material on the rural Aran Islands, pressing his ear to a hole in the floor of his boardinghouse room and listening to the gossip of the kitchen help below.

In spite of his fame, Synge has, probably, the most commonly mispronounced surname in Irish literary history. As another playwright, Lennox Robinson, put it: "You *sing* Synge. You *singe* a cat!" Not an animal-friendly sentiment, but an easy one to remember.

Synge was born April 16, 1871, in Rathfarnham. His father, John Hatch Synge, was a lawyer; he died while John was only a baby. His mother, Kathleen Traill Synge, was the daughter of a Protestant minister. Even in childhood, the young John suffered from asthma and a tubercular condition that would cause him more problems as an adult.

After graduating from Trinity College in Dublin in 1892, Synge traveled to Germany with the intention of studying the violin. When that interest dwindled, he moved on to Paris, where he met William Butler Yeats in 1896. Yeats encouraged Synge in his writing, suggesting that he study Irish folklore and the rural populations of Ireland's Aran Islands to garner material.

Fortunately for the literary world, Synge took his advice. He spent the summers of 1899 to 1902 on the Aran Islands, among the farmers, fishermen, and country folk for whom he held an enormous amount of respect and affection. As he watched them scratch a living from the rough soil or wrestle the raging sea for a meal, he compared his own colorless city existence with theirs and found his world wanting. His plays were filled with the picturesque dialogue, witticisms, and simple but profound wisdom of the noble peasantry.

His first play, *The Shadow of the Glen,* was produced by the Irish National Theatre in 1903 and received outraged reviews. One newspaper claimed it was "an insult to every decent woman in Ireland." Synge's characters were not paragons of virtue; the story portrayed a young woman who did the unthinkable: she committed adultery.

In 1904 Synge became a codirector of the Abbey Theatre, along with W. B. Yeats and Lady Gregory. That same year the Abbey produced his tragic play *Riders to the Sea,* about a woman who loses most of her family to the ocean. Audiences and critics still objected to his work; once again, they felt the realistic treatment of his characters insulted and ridiculed the Irish.

But those problems were nothing compared to the furor caused by Synge's *The Playboy of the Western World.* Audiences literally rioted. In *Playboy,* a young man boasted of killing his father, and a female was far more sexually uninhibited than was acceptable. Also, there were complaints about the "foul" language used—specifically, the word "shift," an old-fashioned term for a woman's undergarment similar to a slip.

During one of the melees, Yeats approached Synge and said, "A young doctor has just told me that he can hardly keep himself from jumping onto a seat and pointing out in that howling mob those whom he is treating for venereal disease."

Synge's last work, *Deirdre of the Sorrows,* was unfinished at the time of his death from Hodgkin's disease on March 24, 1909, at the age of thirty-eight. In his last days at a Dublin nursing home, he was attended and comforted by the beautiful and talented Abbey actress Maire (Molly) O'Neill, whom he had planned to marry. *Deirdre of the Sorrows* was produced posthumously.

# 61

# Sinn Fein

(1902–Present)

In the Irish language, *Sinn Fein* (pronounced "shin fayne") means "We Ourselves." It is the name of an Irish nationalist society founded in 1902 by Arthur Griffith, a journalist, and some of his associates. Their goal was to gain Irish independence from Britain, to promote native Irish culture, and to encourage use of the Irish language. With the support of Irish trade unions and socialists, they pressured the British government however they could to accomplish their goals.

One of their most vigorous attempts was the Easter Rising of 1916 (see CHAPTER 69). The British effectively suppressed the rebellion, and they dealt so harshly with the rebels, carrying out systematic executions, that the Irish people quickly elevated their dead heroes to the status of martyrs. Inflamed, the formerly complacent Irish now rallied to Sinn Fein's cause. In November 1918, seventy-three Sinn Fein members were elected to the British parliament. Led by Eamon De Valera, they declared Ireland's independence.

Great Britain refused to acknowledge their declaration, and warfare erupted between the British military and Irish rebels, who were led primarily by freedom fighter Michael Collins (see CHAPTER 70). The fighting lasted for three years, until Britain agreed to negotiate a treaty that allowed the southern counties of Ireland to withdraw from England and form the Irish Free State.

The members of Sinn Fein were divided on whether to support the treaty. Some refused to divide the island and wanted to hold out for a completely united, free state. Others felt a compromise was necessary. In 1926, the former group, led by De Valera, broke away and formed a society known as Fianna Fáil—in English "the Men of Destiny."

Until the late 1960s, Sinn Fein was less active, but it reemerged as the political branch of the illegal Irish Republican Army. Sinn Fein was barred from negotiations with the British because it refused to condemn the terrorist acts of the IRA.

More progress has been made in the 1990s, as both sides have tired of the violence and sought solutions. The Good Friday Peace Agreement, signed on Good Friday, April 10, 1998, was ratified on May 22, 1998. At this writing, the details of the execution of that agreement are still under negotiation, but it seems a lasting armistice and peace are a real possibility.

# 62

# John L. Sullivan

(1858–1918)

In the late 1800s, an Irish-American fellow was the most celebrated, most popular, and most frequently challenged champion in boxing: the "Boston Strong Boy," John L. Sullivan. He was a bigger-than-life fighting machine who would swagger into a saloon and boast, "I can lick any man in the house." And it was no empty threat. In one such unofficial, exhibition fight he defeated fifteen opponents in a row. His knockout percentage was 87 percent, much higher than most fighters'.

Born in Roxbury, Massachusetts, on October 15, 1858, Sullivan fought his first bout at the age of twenty. On February 7, 1882, in Mississippi City, Mississippi, he knocked out Paddy Ryan and became the Bare Knuckle Heavyweight Champion. Later he would defend his title against Jake Kilrain in a seventy-five-round victory. The last heavyweight champion to fight under London Prize Ring rules (bare knuckles, fight-to-the-finish), he later won under Queensberry rules, with padded gloves.

Sullivan was beloved by boxing fans. Men would proudly claim to have shaken the hand that had shaken John L. Sullivan's hand. Many couples with the surname Sullivan named their newborn sons John L.

Legendary for his heavy drinking in his early years, Sullivan gave up alcohol and campaigned on behalf of temperance. He died in 1918 at the age of fifty-nine in Abingdon, Massachusetts.

The immortal John L. Sullivan held the heavyweight championship title for ten years and is a member of the Boxing Hall of Fame.

# 63

# James Joyce
(1882–1941)

Although James Joyce wrote only a few books, they are among the most frequently studied classics in the world's universities. His epic novels *Ulysses* and *Finnegans Wake* remain the subject of literature classes and are dissected and analyzed by the academics as they search for the abstruse meanings and pregnant symbolism Joyce sprinkled so liberally through his works.

Born in Dublin on February 2, 1882, Joyce was the oldest of ten children in a family whose father, John Stanislaus, liked to live beyond his means. As a result of his financial irresponsibility, the family was frequently on the move, nudged by disgruntled, unpaid landlords. The specter of money problems haunted Joyce for most of his life.

Joyce was a slender fellow with a habit of leaning forward as though in a hurry to arrive at his destination. It was said that when he stood bent over at a street corner, he looked like a question mark. He was severely nearsighted, and his eyes went from bad to worse until he was totally blind.

Like many of the great poet-writers of the day, Joyce spent most of his time away from Ireland—in Paris and then in Zurich and Trieste. Of his departure from his homeland, Joyce said, "At a very early stage I came to the conclusion that to stay in Ireland would be to rot, and I never had any intention of rotting, or at least if I had to, I intended to rot in my own way."

In June 1904, Joyce saw Nora Barnacle, a boardinghouse employee, standing on the street, and he fell instantly in love. They were the quintessential odd couple—he the literary genius, she the common lady who, in Joyce's own words, "doesn't give a rambling damn about art." She frequently "critiqued" his work by saying, "Why don't you write books that people understand?"

He and Nora had two children, Giorgio and Lucia. Sadly, the son died young and the daughter suffered a nervous breakdown and had to be institutionalized.

But not even the trials of his life or his wife's denigrations were enough to dim the glaring light of Joyce's enormous ego. The story goes that when he and W. B. Yeats met, Joyce asked Yeats his age. Yeats mentally deducted a couple of years and said he was thirty-five. Joyce replied, "I have meet you too late. You are too old to be influenced by me."

Later, when Yeats was asked his impression of Joyce, he said, "Never have I encountered so much pretension with so little to show for it."

What lack of respect Joyce's friends and family might have afforded him, he remains the darling of the academics. Although many Joycean scholars have spent vast amounts of time and energy combing his works for hidden meanings and symbolism, Joyce said of himself, "I am more interested in Dublin street names than in the riddle of the universe."

Though he was far from home most of his life, Joyce loved Dublin and claimed that one of the reasons he wrote *Ulysses* was to immortalize the city. In case a bomb should destroy it, Dublin would live on in every detail in his novel. Upon sending his collection of short stories called *Dubliners* to a publisher, he said, "I do not think that any writer has yet presented Dublin to the world. It has been a capital of Europe for thousands of years; it is supposed to be the second city of the British Empire—and it is nearly three times as big as Venice."

With the outbreak of World War II, Joyce fled from France to Switzerland, leaving his daughter behind in a sanitarium in occupied territory. And when he died at the age of fifty-nine, on January 13, 1941, it wasn't in Ireland but in Zurich. But his dream was fulfilled in that his beloved Dublin has an immortality of its own, living on in his words.

# 64

# An Irish Wake

Perhaps no other aspect of Irish culture has received so much criticism as the behavior of the Irish at a wake. Irish folk have been accused of being disrespectful to their dead, of engaging in excessive drink, copious smoking, raucous discourse, even the occasional blows of a shillelagh to the head of a fellow Irishman.

Indeed no Irishman would deny that the revelry of some wakes gets a bit out of hand. Nor would he deny his fellow Paddy a fine send-off to the next world without the glow of good Irish whiskey to warm his way.

Hospitality is as essential to the Irish soul as music and dancing, good food and drink, lively conversation, and political debate. So it is only natural that a man's or woman's final extension of hospitality would be to treat friends and loved ones to a party involving all of these elements.

Traditionally, Irish folks planned their wakes for years before the event: putting monies aside to pay for the constant flow of liquor, instructing musicians on the tunes to be played, choosing the garments they will wear for eternity, the wake games that would be played.

Once the corpse was bathed and prepared by the village women, it was laid across a table or bed in the main room of the house. The body was then covered with a white linen cloth and surrounded by glowing candles, as well as plates of tobacco, snuff, and salt. The great toes of the feet would be bound together with string, to keep the fellow's ghost from wandering the countryside and scaring the life out of his remaining relatives and friends.

After the ritual prayers were said, the wailing or "keening" began. As every Irish man and woman deserved to be adequately mourned at a high volume and with great enthusiasm, professional keeners were sometimes hired to take up the slack.

The Irish wake remains an excellent place to down a pint, spin a yarn, do a jig, and weep a bit for the dearly departed, and yes, political debate still raises the ire and the occasional fist will fly. After all, the Irish are a people who celebrate every moment of precious, God-given life; they could only be expected to celebrate death just as vigorously.

# 65

# "A Soldier's Song"

We'll sing a song, a soldier's song
    With cheering, rousing chorus
As round our blazing fires we throng,
    The starry heavens o'er us;
Impatient for the coming fight,
    And as we wait the morning's light
Here in the silence of the night
    We'll chant a soldier's song.

REFRAIN:
Soldiers are we, whose lives are pledged to Ireland,
    Some have come from a land beyond the wave.
Sworn to be free, no more our ancient sireland
    Shall shelter the despot or the slave;

Tonight we man the bearna baoghal
   In Erin's cause, come woe or weal;
'Mid cannon's roar and rifle's peal
   We'll chant a soldier's song.

Composed in 1907, "A Soldier's Song" is the national anthem of Ireland, and has been since it was adopted as such by governmental decree in 1926. The song is almost always sung in Gaelic, the official language of Ireland. The music was written by Patrick Heaney and the words by Peadar Kearney, an uncle to the celebrated poet Brendan Behan.

"A Soldier's Song" became popular around the time of the 1916 Rising, surpassing the Fenians' "God Save Ireland" and "A Nation Once Again" by Thomas David.

"A Soldier's Song" is a march, rather than a ballad, and is most stirring when played by a full military band. Like the national anthem of the United States, "The Star-Spangled Banner" (the music of which was written by the great Irish bard Turlough O'Carolan), the anthem of Ireland can easily bring a tear to the eye of the listener.

# 66

# Trinity College

## (1591–Present)

The oldest and most famous university in Ireland and one of the oldest English-speaking universities in the world, Trinity College in Dublin (known to natives as TCD) was established by Elizabeth I in 1591. At that time, the generous English queen offered a free education to all Irish Catholics, with only one small catch: they must convert to Protestantism.

That condition is no longer in effect, but as late as 1966 Catholics who chose to study at Trinity College had to receive a special dispensation from the Church or risk excommunication. This restriction was lifted as the curriculum at Trinity became less sectarian.

Still, the majority of TCD's student body of over ten thousand students is Catholic, and its celebrated alumni include Oscar Wilde, Samuel Beckett, Bram Stoker, Jonathan Swift, Robert Emmet, and Thomas Moore. Women were first allowed to attend Trinity in 1904.

Trinity covers forty acres of ground that was reclaimed from the sea. None of the original buildings remain; the oldest are the red brick structures that were built in the early 1700s. The façade is an impressive, classical portico with Corinthian columns. In front of the façade on the lawn stand the statues of two of Trinity's famous alumni, the statesman Edward Burke and the poet Oliver Goldsmith.

The libraries at Trinity house the largest collection of books and manuscripts in Ireland, numbering, at the moment, three million. They are given one copy of every book published in the United Kingdom.

The most famous of their possessions is the magnificent Book of Kells. This wonderfully illustrated, aged manuscript is the number-one visitor attraction in Ireland. They also have the beautiful Book of Armagh, a copy of the New Testament from the ninth century, which also contains St. Patrick's Confession. Another of their treasures is a harp that is said to have belonged to Brian Boru. The harp is now the symbol of Ireland, displayed on Irish coins.

In 1967, the college opened two new buildings, the New Library and the Arts and Social Sciences building, both award-winning architectural designs. So Trinity College's reputation for excellence continues, as does its reverence for the past and its anticipation of the future.

# 67

# Samuel Beckett

## (1906–1989)

A not-particularly-humble James Joyce once bemoaned the fact that he had met W. B. Yeats too late in Yeats's life for Joyce to influence his writing. But Joyce did have a profound impact upon another young writer, his friend and sometime secretary, Samuel Beckett. Joyce was considered a leader of the avant-garde writers, but Beckett was even more experimental than his mentor. That ingenuity and creativity won him a Nobel Prize for literature in 1969.

Born in Dublin in 1906 to a prosperous Protestant family, the young Samuel Beckett found his genteel upbringing stifling and confusing. Educated at Earlsfort House, a preparatory school, Portora Royal School, Enniskillen (Oscar Wilde's alma mater), and Trinity College in Dublin, Beckett taught French for a short while in Belfast. At the age of twenty-three he emigrated to France.

While in Paris, he met James Joyce. The two became friends, and Beckett offered his services as Joyce's secretary while the latter wrote *Finnegans Wake.* Joyce was plagued with eye problems and was nearly blind by that time.

Beckett himself suffered numerous illnesses, although most of his acquaintances considered his afflictions psychosomatic, precipitated by his frequent trips back to Ireland, as required by a demanding and difficult mother. Upon the outbreak of World War II, Beckett left Dublin to return to an embattled Paris. He told his mother, "I prefer France at war than Ireland at peace."

Beckett played an active part in the French Resistance during the war, and as a result, he had to hide from the Germans in Roussillon in southeastern France. He began to write seriously at that point, but it wasn't until he returned to Paris in 1947 that he entered his most creative period.

Beckett wrote about his experiences in his innovative play *En Attendant Godot (Waiting for Godot),* which was produced in 1953. It left audiences amazed by the obvious talent of the writer and confused by the ambiguity of its message(s). One critic described it as a play in which nothing happens . . . twice. Some considered Beckett's work indescribably boring and self-indulgent, but its strength lay in Beckett's originality. Beckett was a pioneer, who expanded the theater's horizons for new playwrights like Pinter, Ionesco, and Adamov, the dramatists of the Absurd.

# 68

# The Claddagh, Irish Symbol of Love

Used on everything from rings to necklaces, from brass door knockers to Christmas tree ornaments, the Claddagh design has represented friendship, loyalty, and affection for centuries in Ireland. Recently, this lovely, uniquely Irish emblem has gained worldwide popularity because of its beauty and universal symbolism.

In the center of the Claddagh is a heart, the image of love. The heart is held on either side by a pair of hands, representing friendship. At the top of the heart is a crown, denoting loyalty.

The Irish have two different stories concerning the origins of the Claddagh. Both credit the Joyce family, one of the ancient tribes of Galway, with its creation.

The first tale is the more fanciful of the two: In the late 1500s, a lady, Margaret Joyce, married a wealthy Spanish merchant named Domingo de Rona. When he died, he left his considerable estate to Margaret, which she generously shared with the poor. Thus, Providence rewarded her in an unusual way. One day, as she was sitting in the sunshine, an eagle flew over her and dropped a golden ring into her lap. This is said to have been the first Claddagh, and all others are replicas of this celestial gift.

The second, more factual version concerns one Richard Joyce, also a resident of Galway, who lived during the late 1600s. Richard was kidnapped and sold into slavery by the Moors. When he was finally able to return to Ireland, he became a talented and prosperous goldsmith. It was Joyce who designed the Claddagh, and some of his pieces still exist today; these valuable collector's items are marked by his personal stamp.

Whatever its beginnings, the Claddagh has become a highly popular design for wedding bands and rings symbolizing friendship between the giver and the recipient.

The way the ring is displayed on the hand is also an indication of the romantic status of the wearer. If the person's heart is "taken," the ring is worn with the lower tip of the heart pointing toward the wrist. If one is "available," the Claddagh is worn the opposite way, with the heart pointing toward the fingertips.

No matter how it is displayed, the Claddagh is a wonderfully Irish way to express, receive, and display affection.

# PART III

# MODERN IRELAND

# 69

# Easter Rising of 1916

## (April 24–29, 1916)

In 1905, a man named Arthur Griffith founded the nationalist party Sinn Fein, whose goal was to induce political reform in Ireland through peaceful means, resulting in the formation of an Irish parliament in Dublin. But the dream of what the Irish nationalists called Home Rule wasn't to be.

On September 28, 1912, almost 75 percent of Ulster Protestants signed a pledge that they would use "all means necessary to defeat Home Rule." Some signed in blood.

Two years later, in 1914, a Home Rule Act was passed, but the Ulster Protestants had succeeded, as four counties of Ulster were excluded from the provisions. Sinn Fein and other nationalist groups strongly objected to having their country partitioned in this manner, and civil war was imminent. The outbreak of World War I diverted attention away from the issue when, on August 4, 1914, Britain declared war on Germany.

Many Catholics fought and lost their lives in British armies naively believing they were accruing points with both the Brits and the Ulstermen, credits that could be cashed in at the end of the war at the bargaining table. But a more savvy group of nationalists, led by Padrick Pearse, believed their brothers' sacrifice was in vain. They took control of the Irish Republican Brotherhood, and they and other groups, like the Irish Volunteers, began planning an uprising. As they saw it, England was busy battling the Germans; what better time to strike than when she was otherwise occupied? They solicited the Germans to join their effort.

The Easter Rising of 1916 was originally intended to be a nation-wide insurrection, but communication problems created a disaster. The IRB had arranged to receive twenty thousand rifles from Germany via a German ship, the *Aud*. However, Americans intercepted a message sent from Ireland to Germany. They informed the British, who captured the German ship before she could reach the rendezvous point in Kerry. The captain scuttled the *Aud* and her cargo. The rebels proceeded without the much-needed weapons, but the rising was confined almost exclusively to Dublin.

The rebels' force was shockingly small, considering their ambitious plans; 1,558 volunteers and an estimated 219 members of the Irish

Citizen Army were all they had to win a country's freedom. Their first move was to occupy the General Post Office and set up headquarters. Then Padrick Pearse stood outside and proclaimed the Irish Republic. The uprising was on. For the next five days, the battle raged between the rebels and British forces. The tide turned against the rebels on Friday, April 28, when General Sir John Maxwell arrived from England with British reinforcements. The General Post Office, a magnificent building, suffered heavy bombardment from the artillery and burned.

On Saturday, April 29, the rebels decided to negotiate terms of surrender, but they were offered only unconditional surrender. At 3:30 P.M., Pearse agreed to lay down arms.

In the end, the cost in human suffering tallied 64 republicans dead, 103 British troops killed, and 357 wounded on both sides. Between May 3rd and May 12, fifteen men were executed. Approximately two thousand male and female rebel sympathizers were imprisoned. All were released between August 1916 and July 1917. The Irish of today consider their freedom a sacred gift from God. The price of that freedom was paid in blood and suffering.

# 70

# Michael Collins

## (1890–1922)

Founder and commander-in-chief of the Irish Army, Michael Collins was known as the "Big Fellow" for more than his extraordinary physical size. He was a potent combination of hot-blooded rebel and cool, methodical organizer, a ruthless soldier and a politician with exquisite finesse. He played a prominent role in the Irish Civil War of 1922–23 and the resulting Irish Free State. And when he, the most wanted man in Ireland, constantly hunted by the British authorities, was finally killed, it would be by those who had once been his own comrades.

Collins was born in 1890, the son of a Catholic tenant farmer in Cork. As a young man he made a living as a clerk, a secretary, and an accountant. But Collins was a passionate patriot, and that, combined with his organizational skills, would enable him to rise to the top of the ranks of the freedom movement.

Collins joined those who revolted in the Easter Rising of 1916 and was arrested along with the others. Upon gaining his freedom he continued the battle for Irish independence. Having used his talents as a financial adviser and fund-raiser for rebel causes, he turned his organizational skills to forming a highly effective intelligence system to wage guerrilla warfare on the Royal Irish Constabulary (the British police force). From the ranks of the newly formed Irish Republican Army, Collins chose a personal staff known as the Squad, which conducted a series of deadly attacks.

These attacks culminated in what the Irish call Bloody Sunday, November 21, 1920. Collins had discovered that some Englishmen in Dublin were actually British intelligence spies, so he planned their assassinations. He later explained this decision by saying, "I found out that those fellows we put on the spot were going to put a lot of us on the spot, so I got in first."

At around 9:00 A.M., IRA members crashed into the houses and hotels where those agents were staying and shot eleven of them. Four more officers were wounded. Two Auxiliaries were also killed, and another was shot by mistake.

The Black and Tans, British enforcers of the day, swiftly retaliated. That afternoon they invaded a Gaelic football match and fired into the players and the crowd, killing twelve people. In Dublin Castle two IRA prisoners were "shot while trying to escape."

Violence between the IRA and the police escalated. From 1919 to 1921, 752 IRA soldiers and Irish civilians were killed. By the end of that period, the Irish people were growing weary of the fight, and Collins knew they were losing the war. Even the English were tired of the affair, and in 1920 the British government passed the Government of Ireland Act, which created Home Rule for Ireland. But the island was partitioned, with separate Irish parliaments in Dublin and in Belfast. A divided Ireland was unacceptable to the republicans, but Collins warned them that the IRA was losing the war.

Eamon De Valera, the president of the new Irish government, asked Collins to be a delegate for the treaty negotiations in London. Collins reluctantly accepted, believing the treaty that divided Ireland was the only avenue open to them. When someone suggested to Collins that by signing the document he had signed his political death warrant, he said, "I may have signed my *actual* death warrant."

His words were sadly prophetic. In August 1922, while riding through County Cork in an open-topped Rolls-Royce, Collins was ambushed and shot to death by hard-line IRA members who objected to his signing of the treaty. He was only thirty-two.

# 71

# Champions in the Political Arena

If ever a people had the heat of politics in its blood and was well-suited to the job, it must be the Irish. Political debate is dearer to the Irish heart than anything other than maybe a pint of Guinness, and that's only because stout ale and heated argument are basically inseparable components of the Irish pub experience. Some of the most effective politicians in the world, specifically in the United States, were (and still are) of Irish heritage.

In the years during and following the terrible potato famine known as the Great Hunger (1845–49), a flood of Irish emigrants left Ireland, to wash up on American shores. With them they brought firsthand knowledge of the suffering of a people with no political power of their own. They knew the value of representation in the governing of their affairs. But in the past, political power could be seized only through violent means, and even bloody struggles often proved fruitless.

In the United States, things were different. A common man,

even one with little education, could create a career for himself in politics, especially if he was a silver-tongued Irish lad with a charismatic personality.

The Irish had several natural abilities that made them excel in the field of politics. First, of course, was the Irish gift of gab, which propelled many a lad and lass from a simple municipal seat to a much grander national office.

Another talent of the Irish politician, especially the early ones, was their skill in arbitration. Trying to create order out of chaos and attempting to bring warring factions together at a peace table were duties performed by the Gaelic chieftains of old and handed down through the generations. Irishmen have always disagreed with one another, but they have also been fairly adept at agreeing on what they're disagreeing about—and that is the first step in negotiation.

Also, the Irish have enjoyed the system of democracy, dating back to the ancient Celts. Throughout early Irish history, the chieftains of the individual family tribes (called *tuaths*) were elected by the clan to protect the group from harm and lead them in attacks against other families if necessary (and sometimes even if not necessary.) Electing strong leaders from their own midst, then submitting to those representatives, has been a long-held standard for the Irish.

The immigrants who began coming to the United States in the mid-1800s had little money and few skills. But they wielded a great deal of political clout because of their voting power. Since Andrew Jackson's presidency in the 1830s, the Democratic Party had established a firm foothold in American politics. The Democrats quickly became the voice of the Irish immigrants; Irish participation and contributions have provided substantial support for the Democrats for the past 150 years.

Here is a short list of some past and current leaders who give us reason to be proud of Irish politicians:

John Fitzgerald Kennedy, U.S. president
Ronald Reagan, U.S. president
Connie Mack, U.S. senator, Florida
George Mitchell, U.S. senator, Maine,
    and independent chairman of Northern Ireland
Edward Kennedy, U.S. senator
Robert F. Kennedy, U.S. attorney general
Christopher Dodd, U.S. senator, Connecticut
Patrick J. Leahy, U.S. senator, Vermont
Carolyn McCarthy, U.S. congresswoman, New York
James Walsh, U.S. congressman, New York
Peter King, U.S. congressman, New York
William M. Daley, U.S. secretary of commerce
Richard J. Daley, mayor of Chicago, Illinois
Richard Riordan, mayor of Los Angeles, California

# 72

# Eamon De Valera

## (1882–1975)

Some say the new, modern, free Ireland is a product of the will of one man: Eamon De Valera. One of Ireland's greatest freedom fighters and president of the Republic of Ireland from 1959 to 1973, De Valera had a vision of an independent Ireland. He spent most of the years of his very long life to bring that dream to fruition.

Born in 1882 in New York to a Spanish father and an Irish mother, De Valera was taken to Ireland when still a child. As a young man, De Valera was an instructor of mathematics at a number of universities, including Rockwell and Belvedere. He also lectured for the Royal University at Dominican, Loreto, Holy Cross, and University Colleges. De Valera joined the Gaelic League in 1908, where he met a lady, a gentle beauty named Sinead Ni Fhlanagain, who would become his wife.

During the Easter Rising of 1916, De Valera distinguished himself by commanding the Third Brigade of the Irish Volunteers at Boland's Mills, and he was the last commander to surrender. Although he was sentenced to die, De Valera's sentence was commuted to life in prison—the American ambassador argued on his behalf because of his American birth—and he was released on June 16, 1917. He served in a number of high offices in some of the most active and powerful political organizations of that time, including Sinn Fein MP for East Clare, Sinn Fein president, and president of the Volunteers.

On May 17, 1918, he was arrested, supposedly for consorting with the Germans. He was incarcerated in Lincoln Prison until Harry Boland and Michael Collins masterminded his escape. (Some say Collins accomplished this feat by dressing De Valera as a female prostitute so that he could slip past the authorities. This may be only a colorful rumor, but Michael Collins was known for his mischievous methods, and he wouldn't have been above forcing the more serious De Valera into such a compromising position.)

For more than fifty years De Valera dominated the Irish political arena with an authoritarian, ironfisted approach that worked very well for him—and in the end, for Ireland.

De Valera was a great fan—and player, too—of Gaelic football. He once said the game was so popular with the Irish because of the "hard cut and thrust of attack and counterattack and the sheer pleasure of getting to grips with your opponent." Perhaps his statement says more about his own competitive nature and his approach to politics than about the game.

Prime minister of Ireland for more than twenty years, he met the challenge of dealing with warring factions within his own nation by maintaining a careful balance between those whose tactics involved street violence and those whose efforts were political but hardly less violent.

Basically humorless and dry, De Valera was not a charming man. As great leaders go, he wasn't especially loved by his constituents. But his lack of charisma was compensated for by his being sensible, grounded, moralistic, and purely no-nonsense. And in a paternal way, he seemed to know what was best for the Irish, whether they agreed with him or not. He said, "Whenever I wanted to know what the Irish people wanted, I had only to examine my own heart, and it told me straight off." No one can doubt that he loved Ireland and poured his life force into serving her until he died in 1975 at the age of ninety-three.

# 73

# F. Scott Fitzgerald

## (1896–1940)

Although he led a life as tragic as his novels and his genius wasn't appreciated or applauded by the critics until well after his death, Francis Scott Fitzgerald wrote a number of novels and short stories that chronicled the period of American history that he called the Jazz Age and others named the Roaring Twenties. In classic stories like *The Great Gatsby,* Fitzgerald portrayed the life of the spirit-impoverished rich and their shattered dreams so accurately because he lived in that world himself. Fitzgerald was very popular in his day, though not greatly respected. Posthumously, he has been lauded as one of America's finest writers of the twentieth century.

Fitzgerald was born on September 24, 1896, in St. Paul, Minnesota to a moderately well-to-do, Irish Catholic family. He attended Princeton University but left to take an army commission. While in the service he met his future wife, a quintessential flapper, Zelda Sayre, who would provide the inspiration for his heroines in stories to come. Also while in the army, he wrote *This Side of Paradise.* The novel was published in 1920, when he was only twenty-four, and Fitzgerald became both famous and wealthy in his own right.

His next novel, *The Beautiful and Damned* (1922), was less popular, but his more than 150 short stories sold well enough to support a lavish lifestyle for him and Zelda. (*The Great Gatsby* is considered by most critics to be his masterpiece, but it sold poorly when it was released in 1925.)

Between 1919 and 1934, Fitzgerald made more than $400,000 writing, a large amount of money in those days. Still it wasn't enough to cover the bills. Financial difficulties caused tensions in the family, and Zelda suffered a major nervous breakdown in 1930. She was treated in a Swiss clinic. This provided the basis for Fitzgerald's *Tender Is the Night,* his fourth novel, which, like most of his writing, was a thinly veiled autobiography.

Zelda continued to move in and out of sanitariums as Fitzgerald lost his battle with alcoholism. After a brief stint as a screenwriter in Hollywood, he suffered two heart attacks and died on December 21, 1940, at the age of forty-four. Zelda died seven years later in a fire at Highland Sanitarium in Asheville, North Carolina.

# 74

# Irish Pubs

With its turf fire glowing, its spirits that warm the heart as well as the belly, and the opportunity it offers for fellowship with your neighbors, the pub is the center of an Irish community. Most Irishmen will spend a bit of time—some a lot—in their local pub every day of their lives. Over a pint they will catch up on the latest news, discuss the liveliest politics, gossip a bit, debate the issues, and, from time to time, take care of some practical business, like where to get a handyman's job for the day or a bed for the night. And they might inquire who has a horse for sale and ask about the health of the nag in question.

There is a true family spirit about the average Irish pub. Children come and go at will, usually with a great deal of clatter and chatter. It isn't unusual to see Sean O'Brian's dozen youngsters run into McCleary's Pub, head straight for their father, and climb all over him, plastering him with hello and goodbye kisses.

A particularly small village might have only one or two pubs, which causes a bit of a problem if some of the townspeople aren't speaking to one another. In one Kerry pub, a stranger to the area asked the bartender where he might find a certain individual. In a hushed whisper, the publican told the visitor, "You mustn't mention that fella in this place. See the lad sittin' over there?" He pointed to a grizzled octogenarian sipping a pint in the corner. "He's that fella's mortal enemy, and if he even hears mention of his name, he'll go crazy entirely."

Barring crazed eighty-year-old Kerrymen, you can have great fun, or *craic* (pronounced "crack"), as they call it in an Irish pub.

Most pubs offer music, whether a single minstrel strumming a guitar in the corner and singing "The Rocky Road to Dublin" or a full band in the extra room, where there will be vigorous dancing. You might even see that octogenarian doing a jig with the energy of a twenty-year-old ... but never on the same side of the room as his mortal enemy.

# 75

# Brendan Behan

## (1923–1964)

Born into a fiercely pro–Irish republic family and having spent many of his formative years in prison for IRA activity, troubled youth Brendan Behan had more than his share of life experience to inspire his writings as he grew into an equally troubled adult. He would become famous for his critically acclaimed plays, *The Quare Fella* and *The Hostage,* and his autobiography, *The Borstal Boy.* He would also achieve infamy through his raucous, drunken lifestyle.

When Behan was born in a Dublin tenement on February 9, 1923, the Irish Civil War was ending and his father was in prison for republican activities. Two days before his seventeenth birthday, Behan was tried and convicted of possessing explosives and sentenced to three years' detention at Borstal, a British prison.

After serving only two years, he was sent back to Ireland. About five months later, he was on trial again. This time the charge was attempted murder of a policeman, who had been fired upon several times during an IRA demonstration. Narrowly escaping a death sentence, Behan was sentenced to fourteen years. He served five and was released under a general amnesty in 1946.

For a while, the young Behan painted houses for a living. Fortunately for him, and for the world, Behan discovered that writing was easier than painting houses, and in the early part of his life he was fairly prolific. He contributed patriotic prose and verse to a magazine called *Fianna: The Voice of Young Ireland,* published short stories, wrote other poems in the Irish language, and earned a modest living as a journalist. Eventually, his talent began to be recognized.

In 1954, when Behan was thirty-one, he married Beatrice Salkeld, who would later publish her own book, *My Life With Brendan* (1973). That same year Behan's play *The Quare Fellow* was accepted by the Pike Theatre in Dublin. The drama was a strong statement about capital punishment, no doubt inspired by Behan's own close brush with the gallows. The brilliance of the play's grim humor gained Behan critical acclaim and international recognition. It is to Behan's credit that, at the height of his celebrity, he wrote a wonderful play, *An Gaill (The Hostage),* for a small, relatively unknown, Irish-speaking theater, An Halla Damer. The play revealed Behan's republican dream of an Irish Ireland, his rejection of violent, fanatical tactics to achieve that objective, and his compassion for those caught in the web of ideological conflict. It was highly successful, and Behan was the toast of Dublin, London, Paris, and New York. In interviews he presented the image of a boisterous, often drunken intellectual with a sharp tongue.

Behan had no patience for critics who analyzed his writings for hidden symbolism and cryptic meanings. When asked about the message of one of his plays, he remarked, "What message? I'm a playwright, not a bloody postman!"

He held even fewer pretensions about his drinking, scoffing at those who claimed his alcoholism was a search for self-discovery or the balm of a wounded soul irreparably damaged early in life. His explanation for his frequent inebriation: "I drink because I like the bloody stuff!" On another occasion he said, "When I was growing up, drunkenness was not regarded as a social disgrace. To get enough to eat was regarded as an achievement; to get drunk was a victory."

But the effects of his drinking began to show in Behan's writing. Even in *Borstal Boy,* which many consider to be his greatest work, the end shows the lack of concentration that would mark his later efforts. Unable to come to terms with his disease, Behan sank deeper into the addiction, and on March 20, 1964, at the age of forty-one, he died of complications from diabetes and alcoholism. The illegal Irish Republican Army gave Brendan Behan a military-style funeral with full honors.

# 76

# James Cagney

## (1899–1986)

On Hollywood's silver screen, tough-guy villains were a dime a dozen, but bad guys who were also lovable were rare. As an actor, Cagney created an endearing scoundrel who touched our hearts. We identified with him and rooted for him without guilt or apology.

Cagney was born in a poor area on the Lower East Side of New York City on July 17, 1899. Jimmy was close to his mother, Carolyn Nelson who taught him the importance of virtuous living and hard work. His father was an Irishman whom Jimmy characterized as a "two for one" bartender—a fellow who drank two for every one he served. When Jimmy was nineteen, his father died of a brief bout of influenza. James Cagney remained a teetotaler for life.

Jimmy earned the occasional dollar by boxing. He was a pretty fair fighter, though he attributed his informal victories to stubbornness rather than toughness. Once he fought another young man for three days. The bout ended only when Cagney broke his hand.

Cagney's show business career began in vaudeville while he was still a teenager, and this lad who would become the epitome of masculinity on the screen debuted onstage dressed as a female.

Cagney met his wife, Billie, in a vaudeville revue. After they married, they opened the Cagné School of Dance in 1927. Making money became far less of a problem once his raw, natural talent was discovered and splayed across the screen in such classics as *Yankee Doodle Dandy* (1942), *Mr. Roberts* (1955), and *Man of a Thousand Faces* (1957).

The street kid from New York City dodged real bullets in *Public Enemy, Taxi!, G-men,* and *Angels with Dirty Faces.* At that point, there were no special effects to simulate gunfire. But he disliked his bad-boy image. After all the hoopla about his shoving a grapefruit into Mae Clark's face in *Public Enemy,* he said, "It was uncalled for, and people don't need to see that stuff."

The city boy loved the country and bought eleven acres near Hollywood. Knowing nothing about the mating habits of chickens (one rooster takes care of an entire harem of hens), Cagney stocked his coop with twenty-six hens and twenty-six roosters, so that each hen could have her own mate. Feathers flew, and poor Cagney never lived it down. But James Cagney did find peace in a rural setting. He died on March 29, 1986, on his farm in Dutchess County, New York.

# 77

# Spencer Tracy
(1900–1967)

Spencer Tracy was an actor's actor, a highly skilled entertainer whose mastery of the art lay in the fact that he made the most difficult performance appear easy. When asked the key to his natural, understated delivery, he said, "Memorize your lines and don't bump into the furniture." Audiences loved him, but only his peers, those who strove to emulate him and fell short, knew just how good Spencer Tracy really was.

Tracy was born in 1900 in Milwaukee, Wisconsin. At the age of seventeen, he cut short his education at a Jesuit preparatory school to enter the U.S. Navy. Later, while attending Ripon College in Wisconsin, he performed in a college play and realized his life ambition: to become a successful actor.

Tracy studied at the American Academy of Dramatic Arts in New York City. In 1930 he was awarded the lead in a Broadway production,

*The Last Mile.* His performance garnered him a film contract with Fox Film Corporation. His first role with Fox was opposite Humphrey Bogart in *Up the River* (1930). Five years later, Tracy signed a long-term contract with MGM, where he starred in such film classics as *Fury* (1936), *Captains Courageous* (1937), *Boys Town* (1938), *Northwest Passage* (1940), and *Dr. Jekyll and Mr. Hyde* (1941).

In 1942, at the age of forty-two, Tracy began a friendship and collaboration with actress Katharine Hepburn that would last for the rest of his life. Although most critics considered Hepburn his equal, she credited Tracy for helping her to refine her own craft. They remained close, loving friends for twenty-five years, until Tracy's death in 1967, and starred together in witty comedies that effectively showcased their combined talent. Several of these classics are *Woman of the Year* (1942), *Adam's Rib* (1949), and *Desk Set* (1957). His last movie, *Guess Who's Coming to Dinner* (1967), would be with Hepburn.

A list of Tracy's other film classics must include *Father of the Bride* (1950), *The Old Man and the Sea* (1958), *Inherit the Wind* (1960), and *Judgment at Nuremberg* (1961). Tracy was nominated for the Academy Award numerous times and was the first actor to receive the honor consecutively for two years. He won the Oscar for his role as a Portuguese fisherman in *Captains Courageous* and for his portrayal of Father Flanagan in *Boys Town*. His last nomination, for his performance in *Guess Who's Coming to Dinner,* came after his death in 1967.

# 78

# Gene Kelly

(1912–1996)

Certainly, Gene Kelly's dancing exemplified grace, skill, and agility. But it was a simple, joyous dance in the midst of a rain shower that we will remember when we think of him. A light-hearted, somewhat childlike fellow skipping puddles and splashing with gleeful abandon in *Singing in the Rain* lifted all our spirits and made us feel we could dance right in his shoes along with him . . . if only our name were Gene Kelly.

Kelly was born in Pittsburgh, Pennsylvania, in 1912 and began dancing right away in his mother's dancing school. He first danced professionally in the musical *Pal Joey* on Broadway in 1940. But he was quickly off to Hollywood, where at the age of thirty he made his film debut in *For Me and My Gal* with Judy Garland. He danced in and codirected *On the Town* (1949) and *Singing in the Rain* (1952). His ballet talents were displayed in his dancing and choreography in the classic film *An American in Paris* (1951). Kelly was also a respected dramatic actor, appearing in such films as *The Three Musketeers* (1948), *Marjorie Morningstar* (1958), *A Guide for the Married Man* (1967), and *Hello, Dolly!* (1969).

Kelly's talent and contributions to film were rewarded by such prestigious prizes as the Legion of Honor from the French government in 1960, and lifetime achievement awards from the Kennedy Center in 1982 and from the American Film Institute in 1985, and the National Medal of Arts in 1994. Kelly died on February 12, 1996, at age eighty-three in his Beverly Hills home.

# 79

# Irish Hospitality

From the moment someone sets foot on Irish soil, he feels as though he has been adopted by an entire country of marvelously hospitable people. Whatever the Irish have, they share abundantly and cheerfully.

In 1579, a visitor said of the Emerald Isle, "If you except the port towns, there are no hotels or lodging houses in the island. Every traveller sets up in the first house he meets, and there is provided with whatever he desires gratuitously."

Long before that accolade, the ancient Celtic lawmakers, the brehons, decreed that hospitality would be officially dictated. According to one precept: "All members of the tribe are required to offer hospitality to strangers. The only exceptions are minor children, madmen, and old people." Another law stated: "The public hostel shall be situated at the intersection of two roads. A man must be stationed at each road to make sure no traveller passes by without stopping to be entertained. A light shall be kept burning on the lawn to guide travellers from a distance."

While things may have changed a bit since then, you will have no trouble finding a cozy bed and breakfast, a hotel with a charming, helpful staff, or a hostel full of people willing and eager to "chat you up" for hours. If you are a bit in your cups—as can happen when chatting with friendly Irishmen—they will make certain a warm bed is prepared for you.

If you are a truly kindhearted sort, you will be careful what you ask of Irish people, knowing that they will move heaven and earth to fulfill your request.

# 80

# John Fitzgerald Kennedy

## (1917–1963)

John F. Kennedy, thirty-fifth president of the United States, was, for a short period in history, the crowning achievement of the Irish Catholics.

Kennedy's great-great-grandfather was a tenant farmer in Dunganstown, County Wexford. His great-grandfather Patrick Kennedy emigrated to the United States in 1848, along with millions of other potato famine victims, and became a cooper by trade. JFK's father, Joseph Patrick Kennedy, built the family fortune and power base as a real estate developer, financier, and banker. His other enterprises included motion pictures, shipbuilding, and stock market speculation. From 1938 until 1940 he served as ambassador to Great Britain. He married Rose Fitzgerald, the daughter of John Francis Fitzgerald, who was mayor of Boston twice.

John Fitzgerald Kennedy was born in Brookline, Massachusetts, on May 29, 1917, Joseph and Rose's second son. In 1940 he graduated from Harvard University. He became a hero in World War II when, as commander of the U.S. Navy torpedo boat PT-109, he saved several of his crewmen after the boat was rammed by a Japanese destroyer.

After Kennedy returned from the war, he was elected to the U.S. House of Representatives in 1946 and the U.S. Senate in 1952. A year later, at the age of thirty-six, he married Jacqueline Bouvier. They had two children, Caroline and John F. Jr. In 1957, Kennedy won the Pulitzer Prize for *Profiles in Courage,* which contained biographical sketches of political heroes.

Kennedy campaigned for the office of president in 1960, opposite Richard Nixon, and he won by a narrow margin. Kennedy's administration was plagued with threats from the Soviet Union. The most serious challenge came with what has been called the Cuban Missile Crisis.

Kennedy's executive actions during his term greatly helped the cause of civil rights in the United States. He either signed into law or laid the groundwork for legislation that would lead to the integration of schools and the desegregation of public facilities.

In 1963, Kennedy visited Ireland and was cheered by wildly enthusiastic crowds. Kennedy's assassination, on November 22, 1963, was particularly painful for the Irish people. To this day, many homes display his picture in a place of honor, along with a photo of the pope.

# 81

# Gaelic Football

The wildly passionate game of Gaelic football originated in Ireland. We aren't sure exactly when, but it became popular in the 1500s. Back then, the rules were loose and the games so rowdy that they were only a stone's throw from the bloody clan warfare of the preceding centuries.

In those days, a team consisted of all the men in a town or parish, which might range from twenty-five to one hundred or more. The opposing team was a neighboring village. Usually the game began at a point halfway between the two towns. The object of the game was to drive the ball into the opponent's town or parish.

The game is more structured now, thanks to the Gaelic Athletic Association, which regulates the sport. A team in Gaelic football is made up of fifteen players, who are not allowed to throw or carry the ball. They may, however, punt, kick, or punch it. They can also "hop" it—bounce it while advancing, like dribbling in basketball.

The goal at the end of each field consists of two vertical posts and a crossbar. A net is strung behind the goal, under the crossbar. One point is earned by kicking or punching the ball over the crossbar. Kicking or punching it into the net earns three.

Although Gaelic football is played mostly in Ireland, it is also enjoyed in Canada and the United States. New York City has a club that competes in Ireland's National League.

# 82

# Angela Lansbury

(1926– )

Few actors are capable of such a wide range of characterization as the veteran Angela Lansbury. She has portrayed everything from the sweetheart of the homicidal barber in the Broadway presentation of *Sweeney Todd,* to the beloved sleuth in the highly popular, long-running television series *Murder, She Wrote* (1984–94). By utilizing that incredible versatility, she has reached the pinnacle of success in movies (three Oscar nominations), theater (four Tony Awards), and television.

Lansbury was born in 1926 in London to a lumber merchant and an Irish-born actress named Moyna MacGill. The family vacationed frequently in Ireland, and some of Lansbury's happiest childhood memories were of times spent there.

Following her thespian mother's example, Angela began to act at an early age. While still a teenager, she won her first Academy Award nomination—for her first film, *Gaslight* (1944). Her other notable credits include the films *The Picture of Dorian Gray* (1945) and *The Manchurian Candidate* (1962) and the stage presentations for which she won Tony Awards: *Mame* (1966), *Dear World* (1969), *Gypsy* (1974), and *Sweeney Todd* (1979).

But with the pinnacles, personal and professional, came valleys. In 1960, Lansbury's beautiful home in Malibu, California, was destroyed by fire. Seeking the healing peace she had experienced as a child on the Emerald Isle, Lansbury moved her family to Ireland. Currently, her primary residence is in Los Angeles, but she still visits Ireland whenever possible, enjoying quiet respite in her cottage there beside the sea.

# 83

# Irish Setters

One of the most beautiful and good-natured of all sporting-breed dogs is the Irish setter. With its long, flowing red coat, graceful limbs, and soulful brown eyes, the animal is lovely, but it also serves well in bird hunting.

The breed originated in Ireland several hundred years ago. Although its progenitors aren't known for certain, it is believed they came from a mixture of the Irish water spaniel and the Irish terrier. Other possibilities include the English setter, Gordon setter, pointer, or spaniel.

Irish setters have long, lean bodies and heads, as well as strong, sinewy legs. They are fairly large dogs, reaching a height of twenty-six inches (sixty-nine centimeters) at the shoulder and weighing about seventy pounds (thirty-two kilograms). Their floppy ears and round, sweet eyes give them lovable faces. But it is their coat that lends them their distinctive beauty. They range in color from a deep mahogany to a golden chestnut, and their long fur flows and ripples when they move. The fringe on the backs of their legs, sometimes called "feathering," and the fan of their tail give them the look of a lady with a billowing petticoat. When they are particularly pleased with themselves, which is often, they prance like circus ponies.

The Irish setter first arrived in the United States in the late 1800s and is now quite popular, due to its kindly disposition. Vigorous and hardy, Irish setters are long-lived and make excellent show animals, as well as pets for families with children.

# 84

# Grace Kelly

(1929–1982)

Grace Kelly was the epitome of elegance and charm. An Academy Award–winning movie star, princess of Monaco, humanitarian, and champion of the arts, Grace played many roles, on-screen and in her personal life.

The third of four children, Grace Patricia Kelly was born in Philadelphia on November 12, 1929, to Margaret and Jack Kelly. Grace adored her bigger-than-life father, a self-made tycoon who had begun life in poverty.

Grace also idolized her uncle George Kelly, a playwright who won a Pulitzer Prize in 1926. Her other heroes included her aunt Grace—for whom she was named—and uncle Walter, both vaudeville performers. From this Irish tradition of humor and entertainment, it was little wonder that Grace decided to pursue a career in acting. At the age of eighteen she entered the American Academy of Dramatic Arts in New York City. Landing important parts proved no problem for the cool, blue-eyed, golden-haired beauty. The studios kept her busy, casting her in such classics as *High Noon* (1952), *Dial M for Murder* (1954), *Rear Window* (1954), *The Bridges at Toko-Ri* (1954), *To Catch a Thief* (1955), *High Society* (1956), and *Country Girl* (1954), for which she won the Oscar for Best Actress.

Grace Kelly met Prince Rainier, the reigning monarch of Monaco on May 6, 1955; the two were married in regal splendor on January 5, 1956. Princess Grace and Prince Rainier had three children: Princess Caroline, Prince Albert, and Princess Stephanie.

The tiny principality of Monaco thrived during Grace's reign. She worked tirelessly, promoting theater, art, and ballet, and her presence brought a great deal of prestige to the region.

But the citizens of Monaco would lose their princess to an untimely death. On September 18, 1982, Grace and her daughter Stephanie were involved in a tragic automobile accident on the winding mountain roads of Monaco. The car, driven by Grace, plunged over a cliff. Stephanie survived without serious injury, but Princess Grace did not. The world mourned her loss, but she left the legacy of her films, her philanthropic works, and her children. She will be remembered with affection and respect, an example of gracious Irish womanhood.

# 85

# Ronald Wilson Reagan

## (1911– )

The prime example of an Irish-American who pulled himself to the top by his "bootstraps," this movie cowboy turned politician used his charisma, wit, and wisdom to become the fortieth president of the United States of America.

Ronald Reagan was born on February 6, 1911, in Tampico, Illinois, above the store where his father was a shoe salesman. His great-grandfather was from Ballyporeen, County Tipperary, Ireland, a place Reagan would visit in 1984 as U.S. president.

Reagan graduated from Eureka College and became a radio sports announcer, with his eye on a career as a Hollywood actor. His dream was realized in 1937 when he received a contract with Warner Brothers. In the next fifteen years, he appeared in fifty films and became one of the most popular actors of his day. He served as president of the Screen

Actors Guild, then worked for eight years as a public relations representative for General Electric. In 1952, at the age of forty-one, he married Nancy Davis. The young actress held the same conservative philosophy as her new husband, as well as his ambitions, which had turned from acting to politics.

Reagan was elected governor of California in 1966 and tried—unsuccessfully, due to an unsupportive legislature—to lower taxes and reduce the size and cost of state government. However, the charming Irishman had learned the value of the media in gaining popular support.

In 1980, Reagan ran for president and won on a platform that emphasized strong national defense, a hard-line stand against the Soviets, and the reduction of the cost and size of government. He also promised a reduction in inflation. During Reagan's first term, inflation and interest rates declined, although the national debt rose sharply, and he was reelected in 1984.

Most historians consider the high point of Reagan's administration to be the treaties between the United States and the Soviet Union during his last term.

Like his Irish-American predecessor, John Kennedy, Reagan was the victim of a shooting, but Reagan survived his wounds. His Irish wit asserted itself as he told the surgeons who were attending him, "I hope you're all Republicans!" The gracious reply: "We are today, sir."

# 86

# James Galway

## (1939– )

"An unusually sweet tone, spectacular agility, devilish merriment, with a springy rhythm" . . . those are the words the music critics use to describe the incredible silver tones coming from the golden flute of the Pied Piper himself, James Galway. From the moment the five-foot, four-inch, stocky fellow with black curly hair and a twinkle in his eye swaggers onstage, his custom-made 18-karat gold flute slung onto his shoulder like a rifle, the audience is mesmerized.

The eldest son of James Galway, a shipyard riveter, and Ethel Steward Galway, a textile mill worker, James Galway was born on December 8, 1939, in Belfast, in what he described as "a workless class" neighborhood. The young Galway was surrounded by family musicians. His mother was a self-taught pianist, his father an accordionist and flutist, his paternal grandfather and uncle also flutists. Galway's first instrument was a harmonica, then a violin. But when he discovered the flute, his life path was set.

He practiced eight hours a day for the sheer joy of playing. When he was only ten, he competed in the Irish Flute Championships, winning three first prizes in solo competitions.

Aided by scholarships, Galway studied at some of the best schools— the Royal College of Music and Guildhall School in London, and the Paris Conservatoire—under some of the most prestigious teachers— Jean Pierre Rampal, Geoffrey Gilbert, and Marcel Moyse. But while he credited his instructors with helping him develop his own unique style, Galway wasn't the best student of music theory, which he irreverently called "codswallop."

Having played with such orchestras as Sadler's Wells Opera, Covent Garden Opera, the London Symphony, the Royal Philharmonic, and the Berlin Philharmonic, Galway decided to go solo in 1975. He plays to sold-out audiences, delighting them with a repertoire that includes crowd-pleasers as diverse as Mozart flute concertos, John Denver's "Annie's Song," Vivaldi's "The Four Seasons," "Humoresque," "The Flight of the Bumblebee," and romantic pieces by Schubert.

Galway lives in Lucerne, Switzerland, with his wife, Anna Christine Renggli, and their three children. When he takes a break from touring, relaxing at home with the family, the modern-day Pied Piper plays piccolo with a local marching band.

# 87

# Mary Higgins Clark
(1931– )

At almost any time, a glance at the fiction bestseller list will reveal a title by the prolific thriller-chiller writer Mary Higgins Clark. The reigning queen of her genre, Clark has amassed seventeen bestsellers to her credit. Her first book, the highly successful *Where Are the Children?*, had been rejected by publishers forty times before its acceptance, but Clark has no fear of rejection slips from editors now. Her fans—millions of them—eagerly anticipate the next Mary Higgins Clark novel, and, considering her voluminous output, they seldom have long to wait.

Born on December 24, 1931, in New York City to an Irish immigrant father from Roscommon, Clark was raised in the Bronx, near Fordham University, which she later attended. In this borough of New York City, the young Mary was surrounded by colorful Irish personalities, whom she credits with influencing her popular writing style.

When asked where she gets the ideas for her rather macabre plots, Clark admits to spending hours in courtrooms, listening to testimony in sensational trials. She says she hears and sees amazing things she would never be able to conjure in her own imagination. One example she gives is the trial of a defendant accused of strangling a woman to death. The prosecutor's closing remarks described in lurid detail how the defendant (who had abnormally long fingers and thumbs) had wrapped those hands around his victim's throat and squeezed until her life was gone. Clark glanced across the room at the defendant and saw that he had hidden his hands under the table, where he was reenacting the strangling, a ghoulish half-smile on his face.

That sort of detail, along with feverishly paced plots, is what gives Clark's stories their chilling authenticity. But although her books are mysteries, her success isn't. A few of her bestsellers include *You Belong to Me* (1998), *All Around the Town* (1992), *Stillwatch* (1984), and *A Stranger Is Watching* (1978).

But life hasn't always been easy for this courageous lady. She became a widow at the age of thirty-three, when her husband, Warren Clark, died of a heart attack, leaving her to raise five children alone. Mary supported herself and her family by writing material for radio programs. Her daughter Carol Higgins Clark is now a successful author in her own right, a fact that delights Mary.

# 88

# Makem and Clancy

(1932– ) (1936– )

Thanks to the talents of Liam Clancy and Tommy Makem, a whole new generation has been introduced to traditional Irish music. Most people can distinctly recall the moment they first heard Tommy Makem sing his beautiful, now-classic "Four Green Fields," or Liam Clancy render his version of the poignant ballad "The Band Played Waltzing Matilda."

Liam Clancy was born in 1936 in Carrick-on-Suir, County Tipperary, into a family of nine children. In 1955, at the age of nineteen, Clancy emigrated to the United States, a young lad who could sing a fine tune and play a little guitar, having already performed with a group in Carrick. But before he left Ireland, Clancy met his future partner, Tommy Makem, through a mutual friend, Diane Hamilton. The two became friends and emigrated within weeks of each other.

The other half of the talented duo, Tommy Makem, was born in

1932 in Keady, County Armagh. Upon emigrating at the age of twenty-three, he settled in Dover, New Hampshire, a town that had a large number of Irish from his hometown. He got a job in a steel plant, where he had a serious accident; his hand was crushed by two tons of steel. While his injury was mending, he visited New York, where he ran into Liam. They formed a duo, joined once in a while by Liam's brothers Tom and Pat. At that time, Pat Clancy was forming Tradition Records. Liam, Tommy, and Pat recorded their first album, *The Rising of the Moon,* which was quickly followed by a second album of drinking songs.

One of the first times they performed, Liam placed the capo on the wrong spot on his guitar neck on their very first song, and they found themselves singing the stirring, masculine, battle song "O'Donnell Abu" in a high soprano. Tommy turned to Liam and said, "You can keep goin' if you like, but I'm not singin' in *that* bloody key!" The audience laughed, they relaxed, and the rest of the evening went well—as did their career from that day forth.

They still play together from time to time. And whether they appear as Makem and Clancy (Tommy and Liam) or as the Clancy Brothers and Tommy Makem (Tommy and some combination of Clancy boys), they are warmly accepted by an audience that is enthralled with their moving ballads and their rollicking tunes.

# 89

# Irish Kindness

Since days of old, Irish hospitality has been a deeply ingrained aspect of the culture (see CHAPTER 79). Kindness to strangers who arrived at your door was not only expected, it was the law. Innkeepers were required to keep a certain amount of food and drink ready at all times to feed hungry strangers who might be dropping by unexpectedly.

One of the brehon laws stated: "The chieftain of the public hostel shall hold open house at all times for unexpected kings, bishops, poets, judges, and all other strangers. No fee shall be charged for bed or board, for the lands and cattle of every hostel are subsidized by the king."

With the arrival of Christianity in the Emerald Isle, the custom of hospitality became even more important, because the folk considered every visitor at their door to be a symbol of Christ, and extending kindness toward a guest was the same as administering to the Lord Himself.

Irish kindness is not reserved for strangers alone. It is an integral part of family life, specifically between younger people and their elders.

Irish children are taught from an early age to be respectful and considerate of their parents, grandparents, uncles, and aunts. It isn't unusual to see three generations living peacefully under one roof, as most of the elderly are lovingly cared for by their children and grandchildren. Most Irish would never consider sending "Ma" or "Da" away for institutional care in their old age.

The Irish are also touchingly compassionate when it comes to those who are mentally ill or challenged. Most villages and towns have one or more of these people whom the Irish call "innocents" or "naturals." And the entire community is aware of and sensitive to their special needs, supplying odd jobs for them to do, and looking out for their safety and general well-being.

If an Irish person heartily dislikes another, he may complain about what he views as character deficiencies. But he would put his differences aside if his neighbor were truly in trouble and needed his assistance.

You can count on Irish people. If you are a stranger to them, you can expect to be treated with kindness. If you are loved by them, they will fold you close to their heart, and there's no warmer place on earth.

# 90

# Frank McCourt

(1930– )

The heartrending, hilarious, grim, and delightful memoir *Angela's Ashes* has remained on the *New York Times* bestseller list for more than a year and won countless awards, including the 1997 Pulitzer Prize and National Book Critics Circle Award. The author, Frank McCourt, turned a horror of a 1930s childhood in the Limerick slums into art. McCourt says, "It was, of course, a miserable childhood: the happy childhood is hardly worth your while."

At first glance, the plot seems a dark stereotype: an alcoholic father drank his paycheck before buying food for the children and was absent more than present when his family needed him most. The deeply depressed, long-suffering mother did what was necessary to keep a roof over the children's heads, including visiting the bed of a cousin— within hearing of her sons. In a world of squalor, the McCourt children starved and froze, and three out of seven died of disease and neglect.

As sad as the story may be, it is also unbelievably funny. McCourt tells his story through the eyes of a child, with the innocence, wonder, and forgiveness of youth. The McCourt children don't realize how horribly they are being treated. Like all other children, they enjoy the simple pleasures of their lives; their generous spirits see only the good and not the shortcomings of their parents. Readers feel enormous pity for Frank and his siblings, but the McCourt offspring display no self-pity. They're too busy trying to stay alive.

Once he arrived on American soil in 1949 at the age of nineteen, McCourt worked as a hotel porter and on the docks. After attending New York University, he taught in vocational schools, then at Stuyvesant High, a prestigious school, for eighteen years.

Now, the wildly successful writer has made seven-figure deals for paperback rights, movie rights, and the rights to his next book, a sequel to *Angela's Ashes*. His play *The Irish . . . And How They Got That Way* has been produced by the Irish Repertory Theatre in New York.

McCourt lives in Manhattan, enjoying the money, the awards, and more attention than his schedule will allow. When asked if writing the book expunged the misery of those years, McCourt said in a rare moment of solemnity, "There was no sense of release. As long as you have memory there's no catharsis."

# 91

# Tom Clancy
(1947– )

Only an elite class of authors earn both the praise of discerning critics and the popular acceptance of the masses. Tom Clancy's novels have garnered him both, and the Irish-American writer is regarded as the father of the "techno-thriller" genre of fiction. His high-concept plots, fast-paced storytelling style, and attention to complex, technical details have proven a winning formula producing *New York Times* bestsellers.

Born in Baltimore, Maryland, in 1947, Clancy was educated at Loyola College in Baltimore. Having excelled in the insurance industry, Clancy followed his dream of writing.

When a news story caught his fancy, about a mutiny occurring aboard a Soviet frigate, the wheels of his imagination began to spin. Twisting and embellishing the story, he concocted a fascinating plot, which became a massive bestseller, *The Hunt for Red October* (1984).

In this book, which later became a movie starring Sean Connery, a Soviet captain decides to defect to the United States and brings his ballistic-missile submarine with him. Clancy did such a meticulous job of researching his novel that he won the cooperation of Pentagon officials, who helped him with his subsequent books.

*Red Storm Rising* (1986) is a chilling thriller about World War III, fought with high-tech weapons. In *Patriot Games* (1987), Clancy's Irish heritage asserts itself; the novel concerns guerrilla warfare and the complexities involved in the Irish paramilitary resistance against Britain. In another novel that revolves around the subject of terrorism, *The Sum of All Fears* (1991), a nuclear war is nearly started by Middle Eastern terrorists. His 1993 novel, *Without Remorse,* details the rescue of American pilots who had been shot down behind enemy lines during the Vietnam War.

Other Clancy books include *Cardinal of the Kremlin* (1988), *Clear and Present Danger* (1989), and *Debt of Honor* (1994).

# 92

# Waterford Crystal
## (1783–Present)

The epitome of contemporary Irish craftsmanship is Waterford crystal, the world's most famous glassware. Each piece of Waterford crystal is a miracle of light, fire, and the master craftsman's skill. The very name is synonymous with beauty and perfection.

In Waterford, a thousand-year-old, Viking-founded city of ancient walls and quays on the banks of the River Suir, visitors may tour the crystal factory and watch the making of this fine product first hand.

Since George and William Penrose first opened their small factory in 1783, Waterford crystal has been given as gifts to kings and queens, presidents, and prime ministers. Chandeliers made of Waterford crystal hang in the world's most elegant palaces, and Waterford goblets have graced the tables of royalty and commoners with excellent taste. But the tools and techniques for creating this miracle are much the same as they were centuries ago. A mixture of silica sand, litharge, and potash is heated in huge furnaces to produce the molten crystal.

A team of master glassblowers and apprentices work around the furnaces, coaxing exquisite shapes from balls of glowing, hot crystal mixture. Using the simple tools of hollow iron rods and wooden molds, the craftsmen carefully determine the thickness of each piece. This is particularly important because the glass will later be multifaceted according to Waterford tradition. Once the crystal shape has been blown, it must be transferred right away to an annealing oven. Annealing is the process of causing glass to cool more slowly than it normally would from its molten state to room temperature. This prevents stresses, or weak spots, from forming in the crystal that would later cause it to break. The annealing ovens allow the glass to cool very slowly, anywhere from two hours for a wine glass to sixteen hours for something larger.

If you think you might find a bargain in the form of a Waterford "second," you won't. Quality is the hallmark of the company, and the crystal is inspected at numerous stages of development. Highly trained personnel make certain that every piece is perfect, conforming to the strictest standards. If at any point in production an item is flawed, no matter how slightly, it is destroyed.

A team of master craftsmen work with diamond-tipped cutting wheels, creating the deeply cut patterns that have been the trademark of Waterford since the eighteenth century.

# 93

# Liam Neeson

(1952– )

Few actors have the privilege of playing such coveted roles as Oscar Schindler, Rob Roy, Michael Collins, Oscar Wilde, Jean Valjean in *Les Miserables,* and a Jedi knight in one of George Lucas's *Star Wars* sequels. But Liam Neeson rises to the occasion—all six feet, four inches of him. And his critically acclaimed acting has given Northern Ireland, specifically the town of Ballymena in County Armagh, and Irish people everywhere true reason to be proud.

When he came to Hollywood and camped out on his agent's couch, Neeson only hoped to land some sort of job before his cash ran out. Fortunately, enough roles came along to keep him in the States until he rose to the top of his profession, receiving a Best Actor Oscar nomination for his amazing performance as Oscar Schindler in Steven Spielberg's *Schindler's List.*

This imposing fellow with a lilt to his Irish brogue wasn't always the calm, self-confident, sophisticated presence he projects now. Neeson was born in 1952 to a poor Roman Catholic family in predominately Protestant Ballymena, the youngest of four children, the others being girls. Neeson held no great expectations of fame or fortune as he grew to manhood and became a boxer, a forklift driver, and an architect's apprentice.

But then he moved to Belfast to attend Queen's University and joined a theater company called the Clans Players. Neeson claims that acting saved his life. After experiencing the trepidations of the "Troubles" on the streets of his own hometown and the fear of the boxing ring, he was ready for the terrors of appearing in film and onstage.

Neeson's success in the filmmaking industry would later give him the opportunity to "say something" about the problems he had witnessed back home, in his role as Michael Collins, the Irish revolutionist and founder of the IRA. Second only to *Titanic, Michael Collins* has been the greatest box office success of any movie ever in Ireland—a source of pride and satisfaction to Neeson.

During his bachelorhood, Neeson was linked with a number of notable beauties, including Julia Roberts, Brooke Shields, and Helen Mirren. He met his wife, the Tony Award–winning actress Natasha Richardson, when they were on Broadway, starring in Eugene O'Neill's *Anna Christie.* They now live in New York City with their two young sons.

# 94

# Irish-American Cops, Keeping the Peace

The big, burly, Irish cop, sauntering down the sidewalk, swinging his billy club, and whistling "Danny Boy," is a stereotype well founded in fact. Irish-Americans have kept the peace in the United States for decades, in the cities of the eastern seaboard, in midwestern communities, and in the Wild West. Those sturdy constitutions are certainly a plus for law enforcement, but even more so is the Irish temperament.

With an inherited Celtic reverence for the law (see BREHON LAW), the Irish have a natural fervor for legal matters and a passion for justice. They also have a talent for mediating disagreements, a vital aspect of law enforcement. These attributes, combined with the "gentle in friendship, fierce in battle" philosophy, make a tough, sensible, compassionate police officer. And the reading of any police roster, especially on the East Coast, will reveal an inordinate number of surnames with an "O" or "Mac" prefix.

Law enforcement has become a family tradition for many Irish-Americans. In some households, several generations proudly carry the badges of their local police departments. And, sadly, many of those families have sacrificed loved ones to the war on crime.

Not all Irish cops walk neighborhood beats or patrol in squad cars. Currently, the police commissioner of Philadelphia is an Irish native, John Timoney of Dublin. Formerly the first deputy police commissioner of the New York City Police Department, Timoney is fiercely proud of his Irish heritage; he is a real cop's cop, who is an inspiration to other Irish peace officers.

Another Ireland-born cop, Denis Mulcahy, is a member of the exclusive NYPD Bomb Squad. This highly specialized unit detects and disposes of explosives and investigates the evidence left behind in the bombings that couldn't be prevented.

But whether walking a beat or sitting behind a desk, Irish sons and daughters have kept the peace for generations, and we all sleep more soundly because they are on patrol.

# 95

# U2

### (1978–Present)

If you spend any time at all in Ireland, you will undoubtedly be asked by some proud Irish person, "Don't you love U2? Don't you think they're brilliant entirely?" And they are! The Irish have every reason to be proud of this internationally popular, critically acclaimed, Grammy-winning rock group.

Four high school lads from Dublin brought their creative talents together to form a band with a wonderfully inventive sound critics would describe as "haunting, dark, and intricate." The lead singer, Paul Hewson, better known as Bono, has an ache in his voice that brings special poignancy to their lyrics, which are typically Celtic—rich in spiritual symbolism and political subtext. David Evans, called the Edge, supplies the distinctive, ringing style of guitar playing that offsets the deep throbbing bass of Adam Clayton and the driving beat and complex percussions of drummer Larry Mullen Jr.

The foursome tasted their first morsel of success when they won a school talent contest in 1978. After a bout of club performances, they recorded their first album, *Boy,* in 1980. With the release of their third album, *War,* they received international recognition and popularity.

But it was *The Unforgettable Fire* (1984) and the extremely successful *The Joshua Tree* (1986) that made them superstars. The songs "I Still Haven't Found What I'm Looking For" and "Where the Streets Have No Name" defined the U2 sound. Theirs is an appealing mix that crosses generational barriers; widely embraced by all age groups, it is lively enough for the young with meaningful messages appreciated by older audiences.

To their credit, U2 uses its popularity and prestige to support international human rights, and has been praised and respected for social contributions as for musicianship.

U2 constantly amazes and treats its audience by remaining innovative, retaining its charm but changing nuance. *Rattle and Hum* (1988), *Achtung Baby* (1991), and *Zooropa* (1993) suggested a more bluesy, folksy sound as though the group were returning to its underground, club days. The lads from Dublin are, indeed, brilliant entirely.

# 96

# Oral Recitation

Long before the Christian monks brought the Latin alphabet to Ireland in the mid-400s, memorization and recitation were vital to the Irish culture. The poets of old were revered for their ability to recite lengthy genealogies as well as to entertain with ancient stories handed from one bard to another.

Oral recitation remains a valued aspect of Irish culture even today. From an early age, children are taught to memorize passages of classical poetry and prose and are encouraged to recite their store of verse to appreciative audiences in school, at church, and in the home. Stage fright is a rare phenomenon, even among the shyest Irish youngsters. To see an eight-year-old quote passages of Yeats—and actually comprehend them—is common.

In almost any Irish pub on practically any evening, you can hear at least one "poet" perform, even if it is to quietly repeat the lines of his favorite political speech or to sing an old song that has the power to bring a tear to the eye. A simple toast can be long and verbose, wishing the recipient a lifetime of good fortune in minute detail. The great philosophers are a popular topic and are quoted at length. The witticisms, insults, and repartée of Oscar Wilde, George Bernard Shaw, Brendan Behan, and others are appreciated—even when inappropriate.

Psychology researchers have found that memorization keeps the mind agile. And Ireland is full of mental acrobats, tightrope walkers—and, admittedly, a few contortionists.

# 97

# Seamus Heaney

## (1939– )

Not since William Butler Yeats has an Irish poet been able to reach into Ireland's past and draw parallels on her present like the Nobel Prize–winning Seamus Heaney. Critics have called him Ireland's greatest living poet, yet he is a humble, unassuming man.

On April 13, 1939, Seamus Justin Heaney was born in County Derry, Northern Ireland, the oldest of Patrick and Margaret Heaney's nine children. Growing up in what Heaney called "the split culture of Ulster" wasn't easy, but his childhood was happy by his own standard. Some of his favorite memories are of the poetry read and recited in his home. At an early age he was encouraged to memorize passages and recite them for friends and family.

At the age of twenty-two, Heaney enrolled in St. Columb's College in Londonderry on a scholarship arranged for students with potential from rural areas. After St. Columb's, he studied at Queen's University in Belfast. There, while analyzing the Gaelic literature of Ireland, he began to identify with his own Irishness. He studied the "bog people," the bodies of humans preserved in the Northern European bogs from as long ago as the Iron Age. Some of those people had been killed in occult ceremonies, sacrificed to their religion. Heaney saw a parallel to the killings and conflicts of present-day Northern Ireland. As he explained in his thesis: "Taken in relation to the tradition of Irish political martyrdom . . . this is more than an archaic barbarous rite: it is an archetypal pattern."

Some of Heaney's best work includes the prose anthology *Mossbawn; Eleven Poems; The Death of a Naturalist; Door Into the Dark; Wintering Out;* and his widely acclaimed *North.* Critics describe his work as masculine, dead-on, and sensuous in its imagery, involving touch, taste, and smell. Heaney uses half-rhymes and internal rhymes, playing with metrics, creating what reviewers have called "gorgeously crafted sound structures."

But Heaney remains unaffected by all the adulation. After he won the 1995 Nobel Prize, Heaney appeared on *The Late Late Show* with host Gay Byrne. Byrne asked him, "Does this mean that you can write any old rubbish from now on?" Heaney replied, tongue in cheek, "I always felt free to do that anyway, Gay."

# 98

# The Irish and Their Horses

The horse is as much a part of the Irish culture as the shamrock, an ongoing source of joy, pride, and old-fashioned fun.

Horses were some of the first inhabitants of the Emerald Isle, arriving long before man. Perhaps as early as 10,000 B.C., when the water level between Ireland and Scotland was much lower and the distance between the two lands only a few miles, horses and giant deer found their way from Scotland across the shallow divide to the paradise of Ireland's pastures.

Some say there is no better spot on earth to raise horses than Ireland. A combination of a mild, moist climate, lush meadow grasses, and limestone (which contributes to strong bones) makes the Emerald Isle a horse breeder's heaven. Many of the world's fastest, finest animals are raised in Ireland, then transported to Europe, the United States, and elsewhere, where they join the roster of Irish-born champions.

There are still as many as eighty-five hunts a year in Ireland, mostly fox and some stag. Sailing over stone walls, roaring across the fields with a pack of Black and Tan hounds, they are a merry sight to behold

For centuries, since the Celts assembled for their athletic games, horse racing has been a way of life for the Irish. Over 270 races occur across the island every year, and a large percentage of the populace engages in the sport, either actively, through breeding and racing, or only slightly less actively, by betting furiously and cheering wildly. Public transportation makes certain that all can attend the races and join in the fun.

If you want to see some of the most magnificent horseflesh in the world, visit the Irish National Stud at Tully in County Kildare, the home of many a Derby winner and Grand National champion. Another Irish traditional treasure is the Connemara Pony. These beautiful, sturdy animals can be enjoyed at the Connemara Pony Show in Clifden in the month of August.

However, some of the most charming of Ireland's equine inhabitants are those you meet on a road in the middle of nowhere. Whether it is a pony named Danny Boy pulling a cart in Killarney, or a hardier cousin of Danny's dragging a plow through a Cork field, these horses are part of the heart and spirit of Ireland. Always have been. Always will be.

# 99

# Irish Dancing

The great Irish poet William Butler Yeats called traditional Irish dancing "the ice of body and the fire of feet." Anyone who has seen those nimble lads and lasses perform an amazing display of fancy footwork, their arms held still at their sides, can understand Yeats's description. Irish step dancing, as it is called, involves a fury of activity below the dancer's waist, and no movement above the belt other than bouncing curls and a smile.

The ancient Celts took great pride in their intricate dance patterns, performed with bare feet between sharp swords laid in a cross on the ground. Daring and beautiful, these routines were part of the entertainment at assemblies, banquets, or even smaller family gatherings.

In the 1600s, the art was revived—minus the dangerous swords—and taught all over the island by traveling dance teachers who shared the tradition with students from village to village.

Now the legacy is continued through dance schools all over Ireland, in the United States, and in any country where the Irish have settled. Many of the teachers are champions in formal competition, the rules of which are governed by An Coimisiun le Rinci Gaelacha (the Irish Dance Commission).

The costumes are marvelous to behold and are often handmade by the dancers themselves or their families and friends. The lads look sharp in their kilts, shirts, ties, and jackets. The girls wear dresses of satin and velvet, adorned with colorful, complex patterns taken from the Book of Kells.

With the advent of the overwhelmingly successful productions *Riverdance* and *Lord of the Dance*, a new appreciation of Irish dancing has emerged. Accompanied by the special effects and visual spectacle of a rock concert, these shows enchant audiences. An explosion of energy, percussion, Celtic melodies, and themes with pagan undertones, these productions rival anything on Broadway and play to packed houses across the United States, Europe, the Far East, and Australia.

Dancing schools can hardly cope with the flood of students who want to learn what they call Riverdancing. And those who learn the craft have no problem finding places to perform, at both Irish and non-Irish gatherings.

Those who dance and those who watch are rediscovering an ancient pleasure—the pounding rhythms of the Irish spirit and the fury of those flying, fiery feet!

# 100

# The Peacemakers

## (Good Friday, April 10, 1998–Present)

Many have said that reaching a solution to the "Troubles" in Ireland is an impossible task. But those who hunger for peace have accepted the challenge of the impossible and labored toward that end. Contradicting the stereotype of the "fighting Irish," these individuals have shown that the Irish, like all people, long to live in harmony with their neighbors.

In September 1997, after a two-month cease-fire declared by the Irish Republican Army, representatives of Sinn Fein (the political branch of the IRA) met in multiparty negotiations with the Republic of Ireland, Northern Ireland, and Great Britain.

A month later, the newly elected prime minister of Great Britain, Tony Blair, met in Belfast, Northern Ireland, with the leader of Sinn Fein, Gerry Adams. Ongoing meetings, chaired by former U.S. senator George J. Mitchell of Maine, resulted in a draft of an agreement. On

April 10, 1998, representatives of eight political parties reached the historic "Good Friday Agreement." On May 22, 1998, an impressive 85 percent of those voting on the island of Ireland (71 percent in Northern Ireland, 95 percent in the Republic of Ireland) approved it in a referendum.

Implementing the agreement has proven to be a tremendous challenge, especially in such touchy areas as police reform, disarming the militants, and freeing prisoners in Northern Ireland. Several horrific bombings have caused some to wonder if the "Troubles" will ever end on Irish soil. But the peacemakers are determined that a lasting accord will be achieved.

In the opening words of the Good Friday Peace Agreement, the authors declare:

> We, the participants in the multi-party negotiations, believe that the agreement we have negotiated offers a truly historic opportunity for a new beginning. The tragedies of the past have left a deep and profoundly regrettable legacy of suffering. We must never forget those who have died or been injured, or their families. But we can best honour them through a fresh start, in which we firmly dedicate ourselves to the achievement of reconciliation, tolerance, and mutual trust, and to the protection and vindication of the human rights of all.

# 101

# Mark McGwire

## (1963– )

On September 8, 1998, one of the most prestigious and long-standing records in sports history was broken—literally with the swing of a base-ball bat. The six-foot, five-inch, 250-pound Irish-American Mark David McGwire belted his sixty-second home run to surpass the all-time single-season Major League home run record. The title had been held for the last thirty-seven years by Roger Maris, who hit sixty-one home runs in 1961. Many experts in the game of baseball had predicted from the start of his career that McGwire would achieve immortality. In a big way he's proven them right.

Born on October 1, 1963, this slugger seemed blessed with a natural instinct for baseball. He began playing Little League at the age of eight. At his first at-bat, facing a twelve-year-old pitcher, Mark hit a home run over the right-field fence. Through the years he grew into not only an extraordinary player on the field but also a man of genuine kindness and warmth off it.

McGwire has always held a special place in his heart for abused children. In September 1997, he wept openly during his public announcement of the formation of the Mark McGwire Foundation for Children. McGwire credits "being a father" as his main motivation for establishing the organization, which is designed to help children who are the victims of physical and sexual abuse. Mark not only meets with some of the abused children personally but also participates in the Make-A-Wish Foundation, a program created to lift the spirits of terminally ill children.

Among his other professional achievements, Mark was named Rookie of the Year in 1987, when he hit forty-nine home runs, the most ever by a rookie. On May 12, 1998, facing the Milwaukee Brewers, he smashed a 527-foot home run, breaking the record for the longest home run in Busch Stadium history. Four days later he broke his own record against the Brewers with a mammoth 545-foot, bases-empty blast.

All in all, Mark McGwire continues to prove he is a phenomenal baseball player and an even greater human being. He makes all Americans and all Irishmen proud.